LITTLE
LESSONS FROM THE
SAINTS

D0104448

LITTLE LESSONS FROM THE SAINTS

52 SIMPLE AND SURPRISING WAYS TO SEE THE SAINT IN YOU

BOB BURNHAM

LOYOLA PRESS.
A JESUIT MINISTRY
Chicago

LOYOLA PRESS.
A JESUIT MINISTRY

3441 N. Ashland Avenue
Chicago, Illinois 60657
(800) 621-1008
www.loyolapress.com

Scripture quotations are from *New Revised Standard Version Bible: Catholic Edition*, copyright © 1989, 1993 National Council of the Churches of Christ in the United States of America. Used by permission. All rights reserved worldwide.

Cover art credit: cristinabagiuiani/iStock/Thinkstock, Shutterstock

ISBN-13: 978-0-8294-4501-5
ISBN-10: 0-8294-4501-3
Library of Congress Control Number: 2016958342

Printed in the United States of America.
17 18 19 20 21 22 23 Versa 10 9 8 7 6 5 4 3 2 1

Cathy, this is your fault.

Contents

Saints on the Brain xi

How to Use This Book xv

Little Lessons for Teachers xxiii

    Saints by Feast Day xxv

Part One Surrender 1

  1 St. Ignatius of Loyola 3

  2 St. Anthony of Padua 6

  3 St. Ireneus 9

  4 St. Martin of Tours 13

  5 St. Joan of Arc 16

  6 St. Charles Lwanga 19

  7 St. Perpetua 22

  8 St. Bernadette Soubirous 25

  9 St. Julie Billiart 28

 10 St. Margaret Mary Alacoque 31

Part Two Freedom 35

 11 St. Francis of Assisi 37

 12 St. Anthony of Egypt 40

 13 St. Paul Le-Bao-Tinh 43

 14 St. Thomas More 46

 15 St. Mary Magdalene 49

 16 St. Kateri Tekakwitha 52

 17 St. Junípero Serra 55

 18 St. Rose of Lima 58

19 St. Philip Neri 61
20 St. Josephine Bakhita...64
21 Mary, the Mother of God 67

Part Three Pilgrimage...71

22 St. Clare of Assisi 73
23 St. Teresa Margaret Redi 76
24 St. Anselm 79
25 St. Justin 82
26 St. Joseph the Worker 85
27 St. Bonaventure..88
28 St. Frances Xavier Cabrini 91
29 St. Catherine of Bologna 94
30 St. Juan Diego Cuauhtlatoatzin 98
31 St. Thomas the Apostle..101
32 St. John of the Cross 104

Part Four Hospitality..107

33 St. Benedict 109
34 St. Scholastica...112
35 St. Angela Merici 115
36 St. Brigid of Ireland..118
37 St. Hildegard of Bingen 121
38 St. Elizabeth of Portugal 124
39 St. Augustine of Hippo 127
40 St. Katharine Drexel..130
41 St. Joseph Vaz...133
42 St. Teresa of Ávila...136

Part Five Loving Knowledge..141

43 St. Teresa of Calcutta...143

44 St. Catherine of Siena 146

45 Blessed Miguel Augustin Pro....................................149

46 St. Boniface 152

47 St. Peter Faber 155

48 St. Maria Goretti 158

49 St. Maximilian Mary Kolbe.......................................161

50 St. Francis de Sales..164

51 St. Faustina Kowalska..167

52 St. Thérèse of Lisieux 170

EPILOGUE...173

PRAYER NOTES AND THOUGHTS 179

ACKNOWLEDGMENTS 183

ABOUT THE AUTHOR...185

Saints on the Brain

While he was recovering from a battle wound, Ignatius of Loyola asked for some books to read. He was probably hoping for tales of romance and knightly valor. Instead, he received *The Life of Christ* by Rudolph of Saxony and *Flowers of the Saints*. As he read—and reread—these books, he asked himself, "What if I should do what St. Francis did?" Over time, he began to forget about his dreams of military adventure and courtly love and sought to imitate the lives of the saints.

You could say he had saints on the brain.

I, too, have saints on the brain. They are my teachers—they show me how to live as a disciple of Christ. Like St. Ignatius, the lives of the saints inspire me to ask the question, "What if I should do as they did?"

We are called to imitate the saints because we are called to be saints. But here's the secret: we are already saints, albeit imperfect ones, for Christ lives in us, and we live in Christ. The saints teach us how to see that truth more clearly.

Pope Francis reminds us that "always, in every place, one can become a saint—that is, one can open oneself to this grace, which works inside us and leads us to holiness." The lessons and meditations in this book are meant to help us open ourselves to such grace so that we can be living saints.

When we recognize our own sanctity—when we realize that we can be saints today, in the ordinariness of our lives—we can live out the promise of the gospel and realize that the kingdom of heaven is a present, if incomplete, reality.

Inspired by such hope, we can effect change for the better.

Lessons, Not Lives

I do not pretend to offer another collection of saintly biographies. I am not a scholar, a historian, or a theologian. I am just a regular guy who takes seriously the counsel of St. Teresa of Ávila: "We need to study, to meditate upon, and to imitate those who, mortals like ourselves, performed such heroic deeds for God."

Every year in my faith formation classes, I ask my students to research a saint. I offer them print and online resources and invite them to share the results of their research. What follows is usually an uninspired report that includes some facts about the saint, such as when and where he or she was born, when the saint's feast day is, and maybe a few interesting anecdotes from that saint's life.

"So what?" I end up asking. "In all that you read about this saint, what about them inspires you? What do they tell you about following Jesus Christ?"

These are the critical questions that we often forget to answer when we read about the saints. We admire them from afar, like the statues that decorate our gardens and churches. We venerate them; we might pray to them to find a lost item; we might ask them to pray for our loved ones who need healing or protection. But how often do we think of them as active, living teachers? How often do we ask the question that St. Ignatius asked all those years ago: "What if I should do as the saints did?"

In the pages that follow, I offer one small lesson from the lives of fifty-two different saints, along with a brief meditation based on that lesson. As you spend time with a saint, you will learn how to apply that saint's particular charism to your life so you can do what they did, but in your own unique way.

How to Use This Book

You can use this book any way you want!

But that's not really helpful. So here are some basic guidelines.

Spend a week with one saint. Choose a regular time to sit with one saint for a week and meditate on that saint's lesson using the steps provided. Meditate at the same time and in the same place each day with the same saint—doing so helps develop discipline, which is extremely beneficial to one's spiritual life. As the week progresses, you may find the meditation leading you into a deeper conversation with God. Over the course of a year, you would have spent time with fifty-two saints on a journey toward your true self—that is, the Christ who dwells in you.

Meditate. Each meditation is as long as it needs to be, but I recommend five to ten minutes to begin with. These meditations draw on Ignatian spirituality—that is, the spirituality developed by St. Ignatius of Loyola in the *Spiritual Exercises*. By reflecting on our personal experiences and comparing them to the life of Christ and the lives of the saints, we will be able to discern what God wants for us.

Each meditation follows the same format:

- *Centering.* Spend a minute or two settling your mind. A brief Scripture verse is offered to help you calm your mind.

- *Reflection.* The meditations draw on your life experiences to help you think about how to apply an aspect of the saint's lesson. One of the great gifts of Ignatian spirituality is its understanding that God can be found in all things, especially in the events of everyday human experience and the thoughts and feelings that surround them. Thus, the reflections often ask you to pay attention to your emotions.

- *Conversation.* Another characteristic of Ignatian spirituality is the practice of "talking to Jesus." St. Ignatius advises us to talk to Jesus as we would talk to our closest friend. God desires authenticity, so in this part of the meditation, tell Jesus whatever is on your mind and listen carefully for his response.

- *Prayer.* Each meditation closes with a prayer to the saint, asking him or her to intercede on your behalf. Of course, you may substitute this prayer with one of your own choosing.

Begin at the beginning. The saints are presented in a specific order and organized into chapters as follows:

- *Surrender.* The spiritual journey begins when we surrender our will to God's will, when we can say, as Mary said, "Let it be with me according to your word." (Luke 1:38) The saints presented in this chapter provide instruction on how to do that, and the meditations provide practice in surrendering to God.

- *Freedom.* Once we have surrendered everything to God, then we can be "poor in spirit." We are free to begin the pilgrimage of love without carrying anything of our own, except an open heart and an open hand. The saints presented in this chapter offer lessons on developing this sense of freedom to love God, others, and yourself. Following this theme, the meditations are essentially acts of liberation.

- *Pilgrimage.* We are all on a journey home toward our Father in heaven. Yet we can get lost along the way—after all, journeying with God can be like walking in a fog at night. The saints are with us on this journey, and they give us useful advice on how to walk the walk. These meditations lead us to our true selves, that is, the person whom God imagines us to be.

- *Hospitality.* Because we are wanderers, we know the value of welcoming others. The saints in this chapter tell us about the importance of welcoming the stranger into our hearts. These meditations are designed to help you develop a sense of hospitality.

- *Loving Knowledge.* The saints in this chapter instruct us on our ultimate goal: to rest in the loving knowledge of God—that is, knowledge of God that does not come from learning, but through the experience of loving. The meditations in this chapter will lead you to experience God's love in your life.

- *Epilogue.* Our journey is never complete. The two meditations presented here will help you keep learning from the saints until Christ comes in his glory.

Meditation Tips

One time, a friend of mine interrupted me. "I'm sorry! Were you meditating?"

I pondered the question for a brief moment before answering, "I don't know. Was I snoring?"

"No," she answered, somewhat puzzled by my question.

"Then yes. I was meditating."

The slope from meditating to napping is steep and slippery. Similarly, interruptions often disturb what is supposed to be a holy purpose. Experience has shown me that meditation is never free from distractions; it is rarely a peaceful repose or an escape from reality. Rather, meditation is an exacting discipline. The following tips have helped me keep my mind focused and my spirit from becoming discouraged:

- *Find a sanctuary.* A dedicated prayer space—a place where you can be alone and silent—is beneficial. Solitude and silence help you be present to the Holy Spirit as opposed to the concerns of the day. Your sanctuary can be as simple as a chair in the corner of a room. Wherever that place may be, when you enter it, you are telling yourself and others that prayer is happening. You can learn more about the practice of sanctuary by reading the book *Sanctuary: Creating a Space for Grace in Your Life* by Terry Hershey (Loyola Press, 2014).

- *Attend to your mind and breath.* One enters meditation with a mind that is calm and still and breathing that is gentle and free. Thus, the centering step at the beginning of each meditation is designed to help you observe your thoughts and feelings objectively (this is what I mean by a calm mind) and keep you focused on the task at hand without distraction (this is what I mean by a still mind). As your mind becomes calm and still, your breathing should become effortless, almost without notice (that is, gentle and free).

- *Ponder, don't think.* Pondering is the means by which your mind becomes calm and still and your breathing becomes gentle and free. To ponder, in this sense, does not mean to analyze or think about or apply. Rather, the sense in which I use the word *ponder* means "to sit with." During the centering step, you "sit with" a Scripture verse until you are focusing solely on the verse, observing objectively any emotions or feelings that rise up in you, and your breathing becomes effortless. Pondering helps settle your mind and your breathing so that your meditation will bear fruit.

- *Wave off distractions.* Distractions are always present in meditation—ambient sounds filter through your sanctuary; random thoughts draw your mind away from its focus; aches and pains can dominate your attention. Distractions, however, are impermanent things. When you find yourself thinking about something other than the meditation, simply state, "I am _____" and name whatever it is you are doing (e.g., "I am thinking," "I am listening," "I am feeling"). Return your attention to whatever it is you were pondering until your mind and breath are calm, still, gentle, and free.

- *Follow the Holy Spirit, not the script.* Sometimes, your meditation might go "off script" and take you along an unexpected path—that is, you might deviate from the steps that are given in the meditation or add your own.

There is nothing magical about these meditations—feel free to adapt them according to your needs. Always follow the prompting of the Holy Spirit. Feel free to break the rules.

- *Attend to your emotions.* Sometimes you might face strong feelings and emotions that occupy your attention. Far from being distractions, God may be trying to speak to you through them. St. Ignatius identified two types of feelings that can occur during prayer: feelings of consolation and feelings of desolation. Feelings of consolation bring a sense of wholeness, happiness, and peace. Feelings of desolation bring a sense of emptiness, sadness, and anxiety. Identifying your feelings as consolation or desolation will help you remain objective and respond to your emotions with skill instead of letting them dictate your behavior.

- *Attend to your body.* Aches, pains, and itches can interfere with meditation by drawing your mind away from what you should be focusing on. But if the Incarnation teaches us anything, it is that our bodies are privileged places to encounter God. So if an ache, pain, or itch begins to distract you, attend to it—locate the sensation in your body and describe it (i.e., is it throbbing, piercing, dull, or sharp? Is it stationary or is it moving? Is it crawling or radiating?). Look at the physical distraction with kindness and love before returning your attention to the meditation.

- *Keep a journal.* Writing your thoughts in a journal is a great way to keep your focus as you meditate. In addition, journals offer you a written record of your spiritual journey, a kind of map that shows you where you've been. Since the same meditation is done over the course of a week, a journal will help you pick up where you left off and provide a level of continuity. Blank pages for recording any thoughts or insights are provided for you in the section Prayer Notes and Thoughts on page 179.

- *Find a spiritual director.* Spiritual direction offers you an opportunity to share your story with a trusted companion. Together, you listen for the Holy Spirit to see where God is active in your life. You might wish to share your experiences of these meditations with a spiritual director to help you understand what the Holy Spirit is trying to tell you and where the Spirit is guiding you.

Little Lessons for Teachers

In my years as a catechist and youth ministry volunteer at my parish, I have noticed that young adults hunger for quiet time to listen to—and be heard by—God. Just as the disciples asked Jesus, "Lord, teach us to pray just as John taught his disciples," youth are excited to learn new ways of praying. (Luke 11:1)

Through imagination and reflections on personal experiences, these meditations will appeal to older youth as well as students who are preparing to celebrate the sacrament of confirmation. Here are some simple tips on how to use these meditations in a classroom or retreat setting:

- **Pick a saint.** If your class or retreat has a patron saint, you might want to begin with the meditation for that saint. Otherwise, you could pick your parish's patron saint (if it has one). You can also use the meditation of a saint whose feast day falls on the day of your class or retreat. If you want to use a saint who does not appear in this book, follow the template beginning on page 176, A Lesson from Your Favorite Saint.

- **Familiarize yourself with the chosen saint and the meditation.** Read the lesson and a brief biography on the saint. (Most of the saints in this book can be found in *Voices of the Saints* by Bert Ghezzi and on www.loyolapress.com.)

- **Set the stage.** Make a prayer space. Place an image, portrait, or icon of the saint, a candle, and a crucifix on a table. When you are ready to begin, gather your students in the prayer space.

- **Share the saint's story.** Briefly explain the saint's life. Share only the essential information, such as when the saint lived, what the saint is most famous for, and how the saint shows us how to live like Christ. If you have a personal devotion to that saint, share that with the youth as well.

- **Begin the meditation.** Follow the steps provided. Light a candle as you begin the centering step. Read the reflections slowly, pausing after each sentence. Allow a minute or two between steps to give the youth time for reflection. Feel free to adapt the wording to make the meditation more accessible to your audience.

- **End the meditation.** Invite youth to recite the closing prayer together. If you use a prayer that they do not all know by heart, make sure they have copies of the prayer.

Saints by Feast Day

Saint	Feast Day	Page
Mary, the Mother of God	January 1	67
Joseph Vaz	January 16	133
Anthony of Egypt	January 17	40
Francis de Sales	January 24	164
Angela Merici	January 27	115
Brigid of Ireland	February 1	118
Josephine Bakhita	February 8	64
Scholastica	February 10	112
Katharine Drexel	March 3	130
Perpetua	March 7	22
Julie Billiart	April 8	28
Bernadette Soubirous	April 16	25
Anselm	April 21	79
Catherine of Siena	April 29	146
Joseph the Worker	May 1	85
Catherine of Bologna	May 9	94
Philip Neri	May 26	61
Joan of Arc	May 30	16
Justin	June 1	82
Charles Lwanga	June 3	19
Boniface	June 5	152
Anthony of Padua	June 13	6
Thomas More	June 22	46

Saint	Feast Day	Page
Ireneus	June 28	9
Junípero Serra	July 1	55
Thomas the Apostle	July 3	101
Elizabeth of Portugal	July 4	124
Maria Goretti	July 6	158
Benedict	July 11	109
Kateri Tekakwitha	July 14	52
Bonaventure	July 15	88
Mary Magdalene	July 22	49
Ignatius of Loyola	July 31	3
Peter Faber	August 2	155
Clare of Assisi	August 11	73
Maximilian Mary Kolbe	August 14	161
Rose of Lima	August 23	58
Augustine of Hippo	August 28	127
Teresa Margaret Redi	September 1	76
Teresa of Calcutta	September 4	143
Hildegard of Bingen	September 17	121
Thérèse of Lisieux	October 1	170
Francis of Assisi	October 4	37
Faustina Kowalska	October 5	167
Teresa of Ávila	October 15	136
Margaret Mary Alacoque	October 16	31
Martin of Tours	November 11	13
Frances Xavier Cabrini	November 13	91
Miguel Augustin Pro	November 23	149
Paul Le-Bao-Tinh	November 24	43
Juan Diego Cuauhtlatoatzin	December 9	98
John of the Cross	December 14	104

Part One
Surrender

Every journey we take begins with a choice: we choose to leave behind what we know for the unknown.

This is the meaning of surrender. To worship God, we have to leave behind what we think we know about God and enter into a living relationship with him through Jesus Christ. We have to be like Mary, the Mother of God, and say "Let it be with me according to your word." (Luke 1:38) If we want to do God's will—that is, if we want to participate in God's active love of the world—we have to abandon our desire for what we think we want and need.

The saints presented in these chapters offer lessons on how we can surrender our fears, anxieties, and even our dreams so that we can embrace what we really need: God's love.

For it is in God's love that we discover the freedom to be the person God imagines us to be.

1

St. Ignatius of Loyola

1491–1556 • Feast Day: July 31

*"We should not prefer health to sickness, riches to poverty,
honor to dishonor, a long life to a short life. . . . Our one
desire and choice should be what is more conducive to the end
for which we are created."*
—St. Ignatius of Loyola, *The Spiritual Exercises*

We talk a lot about freedom in the United States. Our nation
was founded on the principles of freedom and liberty.

Ignatius of Loyola recognized that our spiritual life is also
founded on freedom. Our attachments to our desires—our
desire for health over sickness, for honor and fame, for
wealth—can prevent us from that which we were made for:
to love, serve, and praise God. This may seem like a hard
lesson—who wouldn't desire to be healthy? Who wouldn't
want a long life? Ignatius is asking us to examine our desires
more deeply and ask the important follow-up question, *Why?*
Desiring health so that I can brag about how fit I am is very
different from desiring health so that I can serve God and others better.

When I look at my desires, I need to follow the instruction
of Ignatius and ask myself this question: Do my desires help

me love God and love my neighbor, or are they a hindrance? If the latter, I need to let them go. I have to learn how to give them up. Otherwise, they will prevent me from saying yes to God.

Freedom from our attachments—those things that prevent us from praising, revering, and serving God—is necessary if we want to do God's will. Discernment requires freedom. If we are going to find God in all things, then we need to be free. And to be free, we need to surrender our will, everything that we have, and everything we call our own.

Loving God is nothing less than surrendering to God.

Meditation: Attachments

In this meditation, you will identify the things you cling to that prevent you from loving God and loving your neighbors. What do you need to let go of?

1. Ponder the following Scripture verse until your mind is calm and still and your breathing becomes gentle and free:

   "Go, sell what you own, and give the money to the poor and you will have treasure in heaven; then come, follow me."

   —Mark 10:21

2. Think about something that you think is necessary for you to be happy. It may be a material object, another

person, or an idea. Bring to mind as many details about this thing as you can.

3. How does this thing help you love, serve, and praise God? How does it help you be a "person for others"? That is, how does it help you be loving, kind, generous, and patient with other people? Pay attention to your feelings. How would you describe them? Where would you locate them in your body?

4. Imagine that you never had this thing—not that it was taken away, but that you were unaware that it even existed. How do you imagine you would love, serve, and praise God? What feelings arise in you?

5. Does this thing still seem as necessary for your happiness? Is it necessary for you to love, serve, and praise God and be a person for others?

6. Share your thoughts and feelings with Jesus. What does he have to say about them? Does he tell you what you need to love God and love your neighbors?

7. Close with the following prayer or one of your own choosing: *St. Ignatius, may my one true desire be to love, serve, and praise God. I ask this in Jesus' name. Amen.*

2

St. Anthony of Padua

1195–1231 • Feast Day: June 13

"Let us keep watch and vigil for the Lord in prayer and contemplation."
—St. Anthony of Padua

I often ask the students I teach in my faith formation classes to write about a saint. Someone always writes about St. Anthony of Padua. Every report explains that St. Anthony is the patron saint of lost items and that we can ask for his intercession to help us find things.

Most students who write about St. Anthony explain why: there was a Franciscan novice who lived in the same community as Anthony. The novice decided to leave the community and, before he left, he stole a book of psalms that belonged to Anthony. Anthony became distraught, and he prayed for the book's return. The novice returned the book to Anthony shortly thereafter.

But there was one student who made a point about Anthony that many of us don't know: Anthony had a deep and burning desire to live for God. Anthony frequently took time away from his responsibilities of teaching theology to the Lesser Brothers (as the followers of Francis of Assisi are known) to spend time alone with God in quiet and solitude.

"It is ironic," my student wrote in his paper, "that the man we pray to for help in finding things was himself lost in God."

St. Anthony teaches me another way to think about the term *surrender:* it means losing myself to God.

Meditation: Lost and Found

In this meditation, you will lose yourself in God's word.

1. Ponder the following Scripture verse, allowing your mind to become calm and still and your breathing gentle and free:

   Your words were food and I ate them; your words became to me a joy and the delight of my heart.

   —Jeremiah 15:16

2. Select a passage from one of the Gospels. You may want to use the Gospel reading from the lectionary, or you may want to use one of the following:

   - The First Disciples (John 1:35–51)
   - The Feeding of the Four Thousand (Mark 8:1–10)
   - The Washing of the Disciples' Feet (John 13:1–20)
   - The Resurrection of Jesus (Matthew 28:1–10)

3. Lose yourself in the passage. Imagine as many details as you can, using as many senses as you can. Where did the

passage take place? What images, aromas, and sounds fill the scene? What did the ground feel like under your feet? How did the sunlight feel upon your skin? Who was present? What did they look like? What did their voices sound like?

4. Pick a single image, word, or phrase that stands out, and focus your attention on it. If your mind wanders, gently return your attention to this image, word, or phrase.

5. Find yourself in the scene. Where are you? Who are the people nearest you? What feelings arise in you as you take part in the scene? Find Jesus. How do you interact with him? How does he interact with you?

6. Find yourself back in the present. What is different? What has changed? What new insight, blessing, or grace have you received?

7. Close with the following prayer or one of your own choosing: *St. Anthony, may I lose myself in God's word. I ask this in Jesus' name. Amen.*

3

St. Ireneus

A.D. 125–202 • Feast Day: June 28

"For the faith being ever one and the same, neither does one who is able at great length to discourse regarding it, make any addition to it, nor does one, who can say but little diminish it."

—St. Ireneus, *Against Heresies,* Book I, Chapter 10

I once confessed to a priest that I might be a heretic.

"We're all heretics," he reassured me. "The problem is when we don't realize it."

Now I ask myself the question, "How can I tell if I'm a heretic?"

I can ask St. Ireneus to help me with that answer. His classic work *Against Heresies* was originally written to correct some of the common heresies of the time, particularly the beliefs of the Gnostics and their denial of the Incarnation. He showed that their teachings contradicted what the Church has received from the apostles.

I do not live in a vacuum. My understanding of how to live the gospel is affected by many different influences: Franciscan theology, of course (I am a Secular Franciscan); Ignatian spirituality, naturally (I work for a Jesuit publisher);

and the examples of the saints, obviously. But I'm also influenced by the philosophy of tai chi (a Chinese martial art that emphasizes how softness overcomes hardness); I refuse to ignore what modern science tells me about God (science is one way we communicate with the universe God created); and I incorporate Buddhist practices into my prayer life (I can learn much from the wisdom of my non-Christian friends).

The only way I can be sure that these influences do not lead me away from the truth of Christ is to test them against the Apostles' Creed. If they fail that test, then I need to give them up.

That is the best way I can think of to avoid being a heretic.

Meditation: I Believe . . .

In this meditation, you will reflect on what the creed means to you. You may want to focus on just a single part of the creed on any given day.

1. Ponder the following Scripture verse, allowing your mind to become calm and still and your breathing gentle and free:
   Test everything; hold fast to what is good.

   —1 Thessalonians 5:21

2. Choose one part of the creed and spend a few moments reflecting on it:

- *I believe in one God, the Father almighty.* Think of someone who has been there for you, watching over you, giving himself or herself to you. What was your relationship with that person like? Now imagine having that same relationship with God. How does this change how you see God?

- *I believe in Jesus Christ, his only Son, our Lord.* List two or three of your values—principles that guide your actions. How will you put these values at the service of others? How do these values reflect Jesus and help you imitate him?

- *I believe in the Holy Spirit.* Who is someone you know who exhibits one or more of the fruits of the Holy Spirit (love, joy, peace, patience, kindness, goodness, generosity, gentleness, faithfulness, modesty, self-control, and chastity)? What fruit do you think this person would say you exhibit?

- *I believe in the holy catholic Church.* Imagine Jesus telling you, "Go therefore and make disciples of all nations, baptizing them in the name of the Father and of the Son and of the holy Spirit, and teaching them to obey everything that I have commanded you." (Matthew 28:19–20) What "nations" surround you today? Who are the groups of people you are related to, associate with, or live near? How can you share your love of God with them?

- *I look forward to . . . the life of the world to come.* At the end of time, God will dwell among us, and we will see him face-to-face as he truly is. But we can still find God in our world today. Where do you find God? Where do you feel his presence the most? Where does God find you?

3. Share your reflections with Jesus. Pay attention to how he responds, and pay attention to your reactions to his response. What does he say to you?

4. Close with the following prayer or one of your own choosing: *St. Ireneus, pray that I may always be true to the faith handed down to me from the apostles through the Church. I ask this in Jesus' name. Amen.*

4

St. Martin of Tours

A.D. 336–397 • Feast Day: November 11

"Hitherto I have served you as a soldier: allow me now to become a soldier to God."

—St. Martin, to Emperor Julian Caesar

When I was younger, all I wanted to be was a soldier. My dream was to attend the United States Naval Academy, serve my country, and maybe, someday, become a famous admiral.

After much hard work and many sacrifices, I finally received an appointment to the Naval Academy after my sophomore year in college. Yet after all that, something didn't feel quite right. I didn't have the vocabulary to explain my feelings at the time, but I knew that I was pursuing the wrong dream. So I left.

St. Martin helped me understand why. Martin was a soldier in the Roman army. On the eve of a battle, he told Caesar that it was unlawful for him, as a Christian, to fight. When Caesar called him a coward, Martin volunteered to march in the front lines without any armor or weapons, carrying only Jesus' name on his lips and in his heart. Hearing this, the emperor wisely discharged Martin from service—he saw that Martin was motivated not by cowardice but by something greater.

Part of me still regrets leaving the Naval Academy. I wonder what my life would be like had I remained a soldier. But Martin reminds me that I am a soldier: a soldier to God, and the weapons I wield are the weapons of love, joy, and peace.

And I now know that to wield those weapons, I had to live out God's dreams for me and not my own.

Meditation: God's Dreams

In this meditation, you will reflect on your dreams. How do you live out God's dreams for you?

1. Ponder the following Scripture verse, allowing your mind to become calm and still and your breathing gentle and free:

   "Who am I, O Lord GOD, and what is my house, that you have brought me thus far?"

   —2 Samuel 7:18

2. Spend a few moments thinking about some of the blessings and graces you have received in your life. Say a quick prayer of gratitude for them.

3. Think about a dream you had when you were younger that went unfulfilled. Maybe it was thwarted by things outside your control; maybe it was supplanted by a different dream.

4. Imagine that dream had been fulfilled. How would your life be different? What happened to the blessings and

graces that you identified earlier? Imagine your life without them.

5. What do these blessings and graces tell you about God's dreams for you? How might these dreams make you a "soldier for God"? That is, how might God's dreams for you make the world a kinder and more loving place?

6. Spend some time with Jesus. Share your thoughts and feelings with him. What does he say to you?

7. Close with the following prayer or one of your own choosing: *St. Martin, pray that I may live out God's dreams for me. I ask this in Jesus' name. Amen.*

5

St. Joan of Arc

1412–1431 • Feast Day: May 30

*"I would be the most wretched person in the world if I knew
I was not in the grace of God."*
—St. Joan of Arc

St. Joan knew something that I too easily forget: I am in the grace of God.

I forget because I would rather focus on my sins—my jealousy, my insecurity, my pride, my suspicion, my cynicism. I have somehow convinced myself that I am not worthy of God's love.

Joan never questioned her own worthiness. Even though she was a peasant girl with no education, no military training, and no connections, she boldly demanded an army so she could drive the English out of France. What other people thought of her—and what she thought of herself—didn't matter. She had a mission, a calling from God, and she surrendered to that mission. What others thought of her—her allies in the French court, the English dukes who opposed her on the battlefield, the bishops who sat in judgment over her at her trial—didn't matter.

Joan's boldness, bravery, and courage came from her surrender to God. She reminds me that God will always give me strength, courage, and hope when I feel besieged by feelings of worthlessness.

This is Joan's great lesson: surrender is not defeat—it's liberation.

Meditation: Besieged

In this meditation, you will reflect on how Jesus liberates your heart from the feelings that besiege it.

1. Ponder the following Scripture verse until your mind is calm and still and your breathing becomes gentle and free:

   He delivered me from my mighty enemy,
   for they were too mighty for me.

   —Psalm 18:17

2. As you review your day, take notice of any feelings that prevented you from loving God, yourself, or others. When did you feel shame or insecurity? Anger or hate? Doubt or worthlessness?

3. Imagine that your heart is a citadel under siege from an opposing army. This army consists of your feelings of unworthiness. What is the battle like? Do you feel confident in your defenses? Are you holding the army at bay? Or do you feel like the battle is hopeless?

4. Now imagine Jesus at the head of an army of grace coming to relieve this siege. Who are the soldiers in his army? Are they the fruits of the Holy Spirit, such as patience, kindness, or self-control? Are they virtues such as faith, hope, and love? Review your day again and look for those moments when you experienced these graces. Are there any surprises?

5. Talk with Jesus. How do you respond to his victory? What will you do with your liberated heart? What does Jesus call you to do?

6. Close with the following prayer or one of your own choosing: *St. Joan, may I recognize God's graces in me when I feel attacked and besieged. I ask this in Jesus' name. Amen.*

6

St. Charles Lwanga

1860 or 1865–1886 • Feast Day: June 3

"You are burning me, but it is as if you were pouring water on my body."
—St. Charles Lwanga

There is a lesson that I have learned from the lives of martyrs.

It's not the lesson of persevering in faith in the face of persecution, even if it means death. Focusing too much on that lesson breeds an irrational desire for martyrdom, as if the only way you can show your love for and dedication to Christ is if you are being persecuted. That mentality leads to paranoia, not joy.

The lesson I have learned from the lives of martyrs is simpler: I should not complain.

Consider the martyrdom of St. Charles Lwanga. He served as a page in the royal court of the Ugandan kingdom of Buganda. Fearing that Catholic and Anglican missionaries were plotting to take over his kingdom, King Mwanga demanded that the Christian pages renounce their faith. They refused, and he had them burned alive. Charles prayed quietly as fire consumed him, only crying out "My God!" at the end.

St. Charles did not complain while he was being burned alive—he didn't wail or call for revenge or curse his tormentors. I don't think that was a miracle. I think it was simply because he had surrendered all he had and all he was to God. The flames didn't take anything away from him because he had already given everything to God.

And while we celebrate martyrs because they died for the faith, we would be better off simply following their example to surrender to God's will. When we can do that, we will have nothing to complain about.

Meditation: Complaints

This meditation will help you not be bothered by the little things in life that prevent you from loving.

1. Ponder the following Scripture verse, allowing your mind to become calm and still and your breathing gentle and free:
   Yet if any of you suffers as a Christian, do not consider it a disgrace, but glorify God because you have this name.
   —1 Peter 4:16

2. Reflect on your past day, past week, or even the past month. What was something you complained about? What was the situation? Who was involved? Why did you complain? Was it because your expectations weren't met? Or because you or someone you loved was hurt?

3. Use your imagination to replay the situation. Observe it from a distance as if you were watching it in a movie. As you watch the scene unfold, pay attention to any moments that might seem like a grace—that is, look for moments where God is actively present.

4. Take that moment of grace and sit with it. Observe it. Pay attention to the emotions that rise up within you. Don't analyze the moment by trying to figure out what to do with it or what it means. Just be in the presence of God's grace.

5. Share this grace with Jesus. Tell him what's on your mind. You may want to give thanks for this grace; you may want to ask forgiveness for taking this grace for granted.

6. Close with the following prayer or one of your own choosing: *St. Charles, pray that I may accept the challenges of my day with grace and humility. I ask this in Jesus' name. Amen.*

7

St. Perpetua

A.D. 181–203 • Feast Day: March 7

"It will all happen in the prisoner's dock as God wills; for you may be sure that we are not left to ourselves but are all in his power."
—St. Perpetua

Jesus teaches us to "offer no resistance to one who is evil." (Matthew 5:39)

This is a hard lesson for me to understand. Is Jesus telling me to be a doormat? Shouldn't I stand up and fight for myself and for those who suffer injustice? I want to resist. I want to fight back. If something threatens me, I feel that I have a duty to defend myself and those I love.

St. Perpetua helps me understand what Jesus meant. Shortly after her conversion, the Roman emperor began persecuting Christians. Rather than renounce her faith, she faced death in the arena. When she was gored by a bull and thrown aside, she didn't resist by running and hiding. She stood up, and, concerned for her modesty, covered her exposed thigh and fixed her hair. When the gladiator tasked to finish her off wavered, Perpetua took his hand and guided his sword to her throat. She knew that if he failed in his task, he would suffer the same fate as her.

Perpetua shows me that it is more important to be for something—in her case, for Christ and his kingdom—than it is to be against something. This is what Jesus means when he tells us to offer no resistance to an evildoer. He is telling us that we cannot be against them; we have to be for him.

In this world, it seems that I am surrounded by injustice. Instead of fighting it, I can be *for* something else—namely, the kingdom of heaven—and pursue that, no matter the cost.

That, of course, requires that I am willing to surrender to the will of God.

Meditation: Turn the Other Cheek

In this meditation, you will reflect on how to respond to threats with love, not resistance. Do you respond to threats as Jesus responded to things that threatened him?

1. Ponder the following Scripture verse, allowing your mind to become calm and still and your breathing gentle and free:

   But I say to you, do not resist an evildoer. But if anyone strikes you on the right cheek, turn the other also.

   —Matthew 5:39

2. When did you rely on God's steadfast love today? Spend a moment thanking God for being there for you.

3. Review your day and identify those times when you felt threatened. What threats did you face? Did these threats insult your sense of honor or justice? Were you protecting your family or your home? Were you protecting your sense of responsibility or self-importance?

4. Examine these threats. How did you respond to them? Did you offer any resistance? If so, what did that resistance look like? Ask yourself if this resistance prevented you from being a generous, kind, compassionate, and loving person.

5. Talk to Jesus about this, and ask him for the grace to find refuge in God's love, not in the defenses constructed by your own will. Take this grace with you as you enter tomorrow.

6. Close with this prayer or one of your own choosing: *St. Perpetua, pray that when we are threatened, we offer love, not resistance. We ask this in Jesus' name. Amen.*

8

St. Bernadette Soubirous

1844–1879 • Feast Day: April 16

"O my God, I do not ask you to keep me from suffering, but to be with me in affliction."
—St. Bernadette Soubirous

The existence of suffering poses a real problem: if God is all good, all powerful, and all knowing, why do we suffer?

I look to St. Bernadette Soubirous for an answer. Bernadette was no stranger to suffering. She suffered poverty; she suffered from poor health; she suffered from a poor education; and after receiving visions of Our Lady at Lourdes, she suffered dismissal, ridicule, and harassment.

Her answer: "Here below, pure Love cannot exist without suffering."

If we love someone, we will want to be present to that person in his or her pain, hoping that our presence may offer some relief. This is exactly what God does: God wants to be present to us in our pain and to share in our pain in order to relieve it.

Unfortunately, I want to hide from other people's pain—and my own. But St. Bernadette teaches me that suffering *is* a sign of love and empathy: if I truly love someone,

I will want to be present to their pain; I will want to suffer with them. God's power is not contradicted by suffering; it is manifested in the compassion that surrounds it. Compassion requires humility, a virtue St. Bernadette had in abundance.

I have to surrender my desire to ignore or dismiss the pain of the world so I can embrace it with the love of Christ.

Meditation: Pain and Suffering

In this meditation, you will bring compassion to your pain so you might be able to comfort others. You may want to use this meditation under the guidance of an experienced spiritual director.

1. Ponder the following Scripture verse, allowing your mind to become calm and still and your breathing gentle and soft:

   For the Lord will not
   reject forever;
   Although he causes grief, he will have compassion
   according to the abundance of his steadfast love.

   —Lamentations 3:31–32

2. Identify a source of physical pain. Where are you hurting?

3. Once you locate the source of pain, describe it in as much detail as possible. Observe it objectively. Is it dull or sharp? Throbbing or piercing? Is it localized or does it radiate?

4. Imagine Jesus gently pressing his hand on the location of your pain. As you inhale, focus on the warmth of Jesus' touch and draw it into your body. As you exhale, imagine that you are blowing out all the pain. Repeat this for several moments.

5. Express your gratitude to Jesus for his comfort. What do you say to him? How does he respond to your gratitude? How might you imitate him in offering comfort to others?

6. Close with the following prayer or one of your own choosing: *St. Bernadette, help me bear my suffering with love. I ask this in Jesus' name. Amen.*

9

St. Julie Billiart

1751–1816 • Feast Day: April 8

"Abandonment gives strength, peace and even joy amidst the greatest difficulties."
—St. Julie Billiart

All the saints abandoned themselves to God's will. That often seems risky, irresponsible, or just not practical. Abandoning myself to God does not seem like a safe move.

But abandonment is not recklessness. Recklessness is when you act without thinking about the consequences. When you abandon yourself to God, you know what the consequences of following God are and you go ahead and do it anyway out of love.

If we take the Lord's Prayer seriously when we say "thy will be done," we must surrender ourselves, no matter the consequences. We must put God and others before ourselves. We must love our enemies. We must suffer persecution with humility and meekness, regardless of the repercussions. And we have to do it all out of love.

How do we do this? By being confident in God's goodness, just like St. Julie Billiart. Julie always experienced God as a loving Father, despite facing many hardships: she was paralyzed for twenty-two years following an attack on her father's store; she escaped persecution from French revolutionaries by hiding in a hay cart; she was expelled from the diocese of Amiens because an ambitious bishop wanted to control her congregation of sisters.

"How good is the good of God!" she would proclaim. Indeed, when we are overcome by a sense of God's goodness, it's easy to abandon ourselves to him.

Meditation: The Goodness of God

In this meditation, you will reflect on your willingness to experience God's goodness. Are you willing to abandon yourself to God?

1. Ponder the following Scripture verse until your mind becomes calm and still and your breathing gentle and free:

   "Look, we have left everything and followed you. What then will we have?"

   —Matthew 19:27

2. We often restrain ourselves from following God without realizing it. At the end of the day, ask yourself these questions:

   • *How have I experienced God's goodness today?*

   • *Did I hold myself back from experiencing God's goodness? Did I refrain from sharing God's goodness with others?*

- *Did I make God's goodness complicated by making myself—and others—jump through hoops before experiencing it?*

3. Spend a few moments examining these questions. What obstacles do you notice? Try to name any obstacles you identify. Do not try to push them away.

4. Imagine your day tomorrow. What would tomorrow look like if you abandoned yourself to God's goodness?

5. Have a conversation with Jesus. Ask him to help you seek God's goodness tomorrow.

6. Close with this prayer or one of your own choosing:
   St. Julie, pray that I may always experience the joy of God's goodness in myself, in others, and in all creation. I ask this in Jesus' name. Amen.

10

St. Margaret Mary Alacoque

1647–1690 • Feast Day: October 16

"I need nothing but God, and to lose myself in the heart of Jesus."
—St. Margaret Mary Alacoque

In the Lord's Prayer, Jesus taught us to pray to the Father that his will be done. This is the clarion call to surrender: I have to surrender my will to God's will.

However, doing God's will can be fraught with temptation. When I try to "do" God's will, I inevitably wind up convincing myself that what I want just happens to be what God wants. "Doing God's will" becomes more about my own sense of achievement and accomplishment.

And then, I haven't had to surrender anything. How convenient. No wonder Jesus also included "and lead us not into temptation" in the prayer he taught us. So what does surrendering to God look like? How can I respond to God's limitless love without reservation? I need to imitate Christ. More specifically, I need to make my heart like his.

How on earth can I do that?

St. Margaret Mary Alacoque tells me the answer: I need to lose myself in the Sacred Heart of Jesus. In a series of visions,

Christ had shared the devotion to his Sacred Heart with her: "The divine heart was shown to me on a throne of flames. . . . and was surrounded by a crown of thorns. . . . And there was a cross above it." The devotion to the Sacred Heart of Jesus helps transform my heart to be more like his: so inflamed with love for humankind that its fires cannot be contained within itself.

Then I will know the freedom that comes from surrendering to his love.

Meditation: Kindling

In this meditation, you will imagine your heart being set ablaze with the love of Jesus. How is your heart like the Sacred Heart of Jesus?

1. Ponder the following Scripture verse, allowing your mind to become calm and still and your breathing gentle and free:

   A new heart I will give you and a new spirit I will put within you; and I will remove from your body the heart of stone and give you a heart of flesh.

   —Ezekiel 36:26

2. Imagine a point of light in front of you, at about chest level, some distance away. Watch that point of light draw closer to you. It grows larger and brighter. Imagine Jesus emerging from that light. He reveals his burning heart.

3. Imagine a tongue of fire leaping from his heart to yours. Your heart ignites. Picture your heart on fire. Feel yourself become warm as the flames reach from your heart and stretch throughout your entire body. Soon, your heart should glow brightly as your entire body burns with the love of Christ.

4. Imagine the light from your heart extending to other people. Watch as they begin to glow with Jesus' love. Watch the light from these people extend to others. Continue until your whole world seems alight with Jesus' love.

5. Slowly return your attention back to your heart and then back to Jesus. Does Jesus seem different to you? Do you seem different to Jesus? Do you seem different to yourself? After several moments, allow Jesus to pull away until he is a point of light. Let the point of light drift farther and farther away until you can no longer see it.

6. Close with the following prayer or one of your own choosing: *St. Margaret Mary, pray that I may lose myself in the Sacred Heart of Jesus. I ask this in Jesus' name. Amen.*

Part Two

Freedom

By surrendering to God, we become poor.

Jesus begins his Sermon on the Mount with the beatitude, "Blessed are the poor in spirit, for theirs is the kingdom of heaven." (Matthew 5:3) What does he mean? Perhaps another way of saying it is, "Blessed are those who are free to see themselves as God sees them, for they will be present to the kingdom today."

Having practiced the art of surrender, we can practice what it means to be free—that is, we can learn who we are in God's eyes. In this chapter, the saints instruct us on how to see ourselves as God sees us. They show us that freedom is not a state of being but a lifelong practice that brings us closer to the kingdom of heaven.

Once we know how to live in freedom, we can begin walking toward God. Without freedom, we will go nowhere—we will remain stuck in a false sense of self-importance.

11

St. Francis of Assisi

1182–1226 • Feast Day: October 4

"A servant of God cannot know how much patience and humility he has within himself as long as he is content. When the time comes, however, when those who should make him content do the opposite, he has as much patience and humility at that time and no more."

—St. Francis of Assisi, Admonition #13

When Francis lay on his deathbed, he told one of the brothers tending to him, "Send for Lady Jacoba, and tell her to bring me those cookies that I am so fond of."

You have to love a man whose last words were "Bring me a cookie."

There is, however, an important spiritual lesson to be learned here: the key to living a joyful life is not to avoid difficulties or pain but to be grateful for the little things that bring you comfort in the presence of great suffering. Francis was able to do this because he chose a life of poverty—a life of complete and total dependence on God. He felt joy not because his life was absent of suffering; he found joy in the midst of suffering because he sought to do God the Father's will in all things.

True and perfect joy allows us to be patient in the face of adversity. It allows us not to be upset when we are insulted or persecuted. It allows us to enjoy a cookie on our deathbed.

This is true poverty in spirit. This is true freedom.

Meditation: True and Perfect Joy

The key to true and perfect joy is to be patient during times of adversity. This meditation will help you identify just how much patience you have in those times.

1. Ponder the following Scripture verse until your mind becomes calm and still and your breathing becomes gentle and free:

   "Blessed are the poor in spirit,
   for theirs is the kingdom of heaven."

   —Matthew 5:3

2. Review your day and identify a moment of joy. What were the circumstances that brought it about? What were you doing? Whom were you with? Spend a moment giving thanks to God for that moment of joy.

3. Review your day hour by hour. Identify those moments that were particularly challenging, those times when you were angry or upset. How did you respond? How much patience did you have? Did anything comfort you in those moments?

4. After reviewing your day, spend some time conversing with Jesus. How can he help you be charitable in those moments of adversity—not only toward the cause of the adversity but toward yourself as well? What graces would you like to ask from him?

5. Revisit those moments of adversity, this time looking at them with Jesus. How does Jesus see those moments? How do you react to them?

6. Close with the following prayer or one of your own choosing: *St. Francis, pray that I may be poor in spirit and always seek the kingdom of heaven. I ask this in Jesus' name. Amen.*

12

St. Anthony of Egypt

251–356 • Feast Day: January 17

*"But let us rather apply ourselves to our resolve of discipline,
and let us not be deceived by them who do all things in deceit,
even though they threaten death. For they are weak and can
do nought but threaten."*
—St. Anthony of Egypt

After reading *The Life of Anthony*—which was written by another famous saint, St. Athanasius—I'm beginning to think that freedom is less a state of being (e.g., "I *am* free") than it is a discipline (i.e., "I *practice* freedom.")

Anthony spent his time alone in the desert outside Thebes, Egypt, praying and fasting. While solitude and silence helped him tell the difference between what is of God and what is not, it must also have been maddening. Anthony was repeatedly tormented by demons; his response was always the same: he ignored them, "for they are nothing and quickly disappear."

Like Anthony, I face many demons: arrogance and insecurity, the desire to control others, my need to be the center of attention. St. Anthony teaches me that I do not need to be afraid of these demons. When they raise their ugly heads, I need to let them float away like the clouds in the sky. They are powerless over me. All I have to do is be patient and remain faithful to Christ—that is, to be kind, loving, merciful, understanding, and hospitable.

In order to practice the kind of freedom that Anthony modeled, we, too, need solitude and silence. Solitude makes silence possible, and it is in silence that we hear God whispering his desires for us.

Meditation: Practicing Freedom

In this meditation, we will enter the desert of solitude and silence to find freedom.

1. Ponder the following Scripture verse, allowing your mind to become calm and still and your breathing gentle and free:

   And the Spirit immediately drove him out into the wilderness. He was in the wilderness for forty days, tempted by Satan, and he was with the wild beasts; and the angels waited on him.

   —Mark 1:12–13

2. Imagine that you are in a solitary place. Maybe you are in a desert, a cave, or on a mountain top. Try to imagine as many details as possible. Is it hot or cold? Is it barren or full of life? What sounds fill the air? Where do you see God in this place?

3. Stay with this image for as long as you can. Your mind will start to drift. You might be distracted by something that happened earlier in the day, feel anxiety about the future, hear a sound that interrupts your thinking, or feel an itch or an ache. Do not judge yourself if you are distracted; you should expect distractions and welcome them.

4. When you notice that you are focused on the distraction and not your place of solitude, respond in this manner:

   - Greet the distraction. Say "Hello" or "Welcome."

   - Introduce yourself to the distraction. If it is a feeling, name the feeling. If it is a sound, name the sound.

   - Dismiss the distraction kindly and return your attention to your place of solitude.

5. Imagine Jesus joining you in your place of solitude. How does he minister to you? How do you respond to his presence? If you find reason to give thanks, then give him thanks. If you feel the need to ask forgiveness, ask Jesus for forgiveness.

6. Close with the following prayer or one of your own choosing: *St. Anthony, pray that I may develop the discipline to keep my mind free and focused on Christ. Amen.*

13

St. Paul Le-Bao-Tinh

1793–1857 • Feast Day: November 24

"But the God who once freed the three children from the fiery furnace is with me always; he has delivered me from these tribulations and made them sweet, for his mercy is forever."
—St. Paul Le-Bao-Tinh

Many saints had a sacred space where they went to be alone with God, whether it was a cave high up a mountain or a small hut in the woods. My sacred space is a corner of my den, where there is a chair with a small table beside it. I will sit there and just be with God. Sometimes I will pray the Rosary; sometimes I will journal; sometimes I will pet my dog (who is not clear on the concept of personal space).

I am often tempted to retreat to this space in order to get away from it all: I want to run away and be with God and tell the world to go and take care of itself.

In some ways, I might be like St. Paul Le-Bao-Tinh. He was one of one hundred and seventeen Vietnamese martyrs (including St. Andrew Dung-Lac) canonized by Pope John Paul II in 1988. Paul Le-Bao-Tinh admired the saints who had renounced the world and lived as hermits. He imitated their simple and harsh life by retreating to the mountains of Laos, living a life devoted to contemplating God's mystery.

But Paul realized that he could not escape the world without abandoning his brothers and sisters. Therefore, he returned to the seminary to finish his studies to become a priest, where he was arrested and sentenced to death when Christianity was outlawed and priests were classified as criminals.

St. Paul teaches me that a life for God is a life for others. I cannot retreat from the world; I have to retreat *for* the world. If I don't do that, my sanctuary simply becomes a well-disguised prison, preventing me from being Christ's hands and feet in the world.

Meditation: A Retreat for the World

In this meditation, you share the graces you have received with the world.

1. Ponder this Scripture verse until your mind becomes calm and still and your breathing gentle and free:
   "Let us go on to the neighboring towns, so that I may proclaim the message there also; for that is what I came out to do."

   —Mark 1:38

2. Place yourself in your sanctuary. If you do not have one, imagine a place that is sacred—that is, a place where you

feel God is particularly close to you, a place where you feel at peace. Pay attention to the details of this place. What do you see? What makes this place sacred?

3. Spend a few moments in your sanctuary. Look back on your day and find a moment of grace. When did you feel God's presence in your life today? Say a prayer of thanksgiving for this moment.

4. Imagine Jesus is with you in your sanctuary. Hand this grace to him. How does he receive it? How do you feel giving this grace up to him?

5. Follow Jesus as he leaves your sanctuary and goes into your community. He hands out the grace you gave him to your neighbors, to people you don't know very well or at all. He even gives it to people you do not like. What feelings do you notice as you watch him share this grace with the people around you? How do they react to this unexpected gift?

6. Look forward to tomorrow. What graces will you need? How might you imitate Jesus and share those graces with the people you encounter?

7. Close with the following prayer or one of your own:
St. Paul, remind me to never retreat from the world, but to always serve as Christ's hands and feet in the world. I ask this in Jesus' name. Amen.

14

St. Thomas More

1478–1535 • Feast Day: June 22

"Verily, daughter, I never intend (God being my good Lord) to pin my soul at another man's back, not even the best man I know this day living: for I know not whither he hap to carry it. There is no man living, of whom while he liveth, I may make myself sure."

—St. Thomas More, in a letter to his daughter Margaret

When Thomas More was sent to prison for not signing King Henry VIII's oath of supremacy, his daughter Margaret wondered if he had been influenced by the opinion of another man, his friend Cardinal John Fisher. Thomas assured her that he was his own man—he put his trust in God and God alone.

This is a lesson I easily forget. Too often I chain myself to other people, people who I think are holy and wise. I may imitate their prayer lives. I may adopt their opinions and ideas as my own (often quoting these people at great length). In the end, I let them influence me to the point where I want to share their experience of God instead of searching for my own. Little do I realize that I have made them into idols: I praise and glorify them instead of God.

To be free means to be my true self—the person God imagines me to be.

The only way I will know the person God imagines me to be is by imitating Christ, not other people.

Meditation: The King's Good Servant

This meditation will help you identify reasons why you trust the people you do. Do you trust them more than you trust Jesus?

1. Ponder the following Scripture verse, allowing your mind to become calm and still and your breathing gentle and free:

   Do not put your trust in princes,
   *   in mortals, in whom there is no help.*
   Happy are those whose help is the God of Jacob,
   *   whose hope is in the LORD, their God.*

   —Psalm 146:3,5

2. Who are the people in your life you trust? Imagine as many details about one of these people as you can. What feelings arise as you think of this person? Why do you trust this person?

3. Imagine what it would be like if that person betrayed you. How would you react to such a betrayal? What feelings arise?

4. Spend some time in conversation with Jesus; tell him why you trust this person. Listen to what Jesus has to say.

Does he tell you that you can trust him for the same reasons? Does he seem sad that you seem to trust this person more than him? Does he tell you something about this person that you don't want to hear?

5. Close with this prayer or one of your own choosing:
   St. Thomas, pray that I may not pin my soul to any other person but only to God. I ask this in Jesus' name. Amen.

15

St. Mary Magdalene

First Century • Feast Day: July 22

"They have taken away my Lord, and I do not know where they have laid him."

—Mary Magdalene, John 20:13

"Bob, what's the difference between grasping and being grasped?" my spiritual director once asked me.

"One is something I do; the other is something done to me," I responded immediately.

I could tell by her scowl (I tend to make her do that—sometimes I think I am her penance) that I wasn't supposed to answer so quickly. Rather, she wanted me to sit with this thought for a while, to ponder it—not analyze it or dissect it for meaning, but to let it lead me into contemplation.

Her question reminded me of when Mary Magdalene encountered the risen Christ. "Do not hold on to me," Jesus told her. (John 20:17) Like Mary, I can also hold on too tightly to Jesus. I like to put him in a box—Jesus would behave this way, not that way; Jesus meant this, not that. Jesus can only love me if I do *X*, *Y*, and *Z*. I tend to love the image of the man that I have created, not the man himself.

That's not faith. That's idolatry.

I think my spiritual director was asking me to imitate Mary Magdalene, not by holding on to Jesus, but by being present to him under the cross (Mark 15:40; Matthew 27:56) and outside the tomb (Matthew 28:1; Luke 23:55–56).

That's where we find freedom: not in holding on to Jesus but by letting go of him so that Christ can be present to us.

Meditation: Clinging

In this meditation, you will learn to be like Mary Magdalene and let Jesus ascend to the Father.

1. Ponder the following Scripture verse, allowing your mind to become calm and still and your breathing gentle and free:

   "But go to my brothers and say to them, 'I am ascending to my Father and your Father, to my God and your God.'"
   —John 20:17

2. Think of a time when you clung to Jesus. Perhaps you were grieving, and you clung to him for comfort. Perhaps you were afraid, and you clung to him for courage. Perhaps you were experiencing a period of weakness, and you clung to him for strength.

3. Imagine holding on to him. Are you holding his hand, squeezing it tightly? Are your arms wrapped around his waist, as if pleading with him not to leave? How does Jesus react to your grasping of him?

4. Jesus says to you, "Stop holding on to me." You let go. What feelings arise in you as you let go of him and watch him ascend into heaven? What do you think God is trying to tell you about these feelings?

5. Imagine that you see two people in white garments. They say, "Why do you stand looking up towards heaven? This Jesus, who has been taken up from you into heaven, will come in the same way." (Acts of the Apostles 1:11) What do you say to them? How do they respond to you? What feelings arise in you? How do they compare with what you felt when you first let go of Jesus?

6. Close with the following prayer or one of your own choosing: *St. Mary Magdalene, pray that I may always look for Christ alive in the world today. I ask this in Jesus' name. Amen.*

16

St. Kateri Tekakwitha

1656–1680 • Feast Day: July 14

"I am not my own; I have given myself to Jesus. He must be my only love."
—St. Kateri Tekakwitha

My life is compartmentalized into different worlds. My work life, my spiritual life, and my leisure life often seem separate from one another. Who I am in prayer is often not who I am at work, I'm sorry to say. The challenge I face is not transitioning from one world to another—this I do rather easily. The challenge I face is having these separate worlds meld into one, so that while they remain distinct, who I am in one is no different from who I am in any other.

When I think about the example of St. Kateri Tekakwitha, I am shown someone who bridged distinct worlds that were not necessarily different. She bridged distinct cultures. She was born to an Algonquin mother and a Mohawk father and was baptized by the Jesuits, though she remained true to her Iroquois traditions. But even among these distinctions, she realized that there were no differences: we are all one in Christ.

Today, St. Kateri inspires hundreds of thousands of Native Americans who celebrate their Catholic identity and yet still want to affirm the traditions of their people. That is the freedom we find in the love of Christ: we can embrace distinctions because we recognize that there are no differences. We are all created in the love of Christ, and all good things come from him.

If I can remember this, then who I am—a beloved child of God—will be the same, no matter which world I travel to.

Meditation: Worlds Apart

In this meditation, you will reflect on your behavior in different circumstances. Who is your true and authentic self?

1. Ponder the following Scripture verse, allowing your mind to become calm and still and your breathing gentle and free:

   "I made your name known to them, and I will make it known, so that the love with which you loved me may be in them, and I in them."

   —John 17:26

2. Reflect on the different "worlds" you inhabit. How do you behave in these different social environments? Who are you when you are at home? At work? At church? With friends? By yourself? What are the similarities and differences?

3. Pay attention to the feelings that arise in you as you watch yourself in each setting. Which version of you feels

like or looks like the real you? Which version of you feels most like an imposter, an inauthentic sense of who you really are?

4. Which version of you is most like Jesus? What are the similarities between the two?

5. Focus on your authentic self, the image that is most like Jesus. How is this version of yourself always present, no matter your social environment? What are the forces that keep this authentic version of yourself from coming forward?

6. Talk to Jesus for a few moments. Share with him your thoughts and feelings. If you asked him to describe who you really are, what would he say? Ask Jesus for the grace to be your authentic self, no matter what world you inhabit.

7. Close with the following prayer or one of your own choosing: *St. Kateri, pray for me that I may be a bridge between different worlds that brings people together in love. I ask this in Jesus' name. Amen.*

17

St. Junípero Serra

1713–1784 • Feast Day: July 1

"By practicing holy patience and resignation to the Divine Will, they will possess their souls, and attain eternal life."
—St. Junípero Serra, letter to Fr. Francesch Serra

Consider the life of St. Junípero Serra.

He left a comfortable life as a professor in Spain to become a missionary in North America. He established nine Franciscan missions in California, including ones in San Diego, San Francisco, and Santa Clara. He baptized more than six thousand Native Americans and confirmed more than five thousand.

Yet his past is not without controversy. To many Native Americans, Junípero Serra was anything but a saint: he was an unapologetic abuser of the indigenous people of California and responsible for the devastation of their culture. His defenders, on the other hand, explain that we have to understand Junípero's life in context. From this perspective, Junípero was a champion of Native Americans' rights, working to help them make the best out of what would have seemed like the end of their world: imperial conquest, disease, and famine.

I do not feel that I should pick a side in this controversy. Rather, I ought to look at Junípero—and myself—honestly. We are not perfect people. While we can certainly do holy things, we might also do things that are unconscionable from another's point of view. We need to practice "holy patience" with ourselves; that is, we need to rest in knowing that God is good, even when we are not.

Perhaps this is the lesson St. Junípero teaches me: What makes me holy is not what I do or how I am remembered. What makes me holy is that God loves me unconditionally. This lesson is the basis of my freedom.

Meditation: Sinner & Saint

We are simultaneously sinner and saint. This meditation will remind you that you are holy not because of anything you do but because God loves you.

1. Ponder the following Scripture verse, allowing your mind to become calm and still and your breathing gentle and free:

    Jesus answered him, "Why do you call me good? No one is good but God alone."

    —Mark 10:18

2. Recall a deed you performed that you thought was good but went unappreciated, had unintended negative consequences, or didn't go as planned. Why did you think it

was good? Whom did you hope would have benefited from the deed and how? Did you expect any personal benefits?

3. Consider this deed from other perspectives. How does it look from the person on the receiving end? How does it look from the perspective of a disinterested observer? How does it look from one of your detractors? What light do these perspectives shine on your motives and actions? Do you still consider them good?

4. Finally, consider the deed from Jesus' perspective. Does it still seem good or does it seem less so? Do such labels even matter? What would Jesus have done differently? What would Jesus have done that was the same?

5. Talk to Jesus. What questions do you have for him? What insights does he share with you? If you feel the need to ask forgiveness, ask for forgiveness. If you desire to thank or praise him, then give him thanks and praise.

6. Close with the following prayer or one of your own choosing: *St. Junípero, pray that I may never forget that I am loved by God and that God alone is good. I ask this in Jesus' name. Amen.*

18

St. Rose of Lima

1586–1617 • Feast Day: August 23

"If only mortals would learn how great it is to possess divine grace, how beautiful, how noble, how precious. How many riches it hides within itself, how many joys and delights."
—St. Rose of Lima

Confession: I'm afraid of being rejected and ridiculed.

I know I'm not alone in this fear. St. Rose of Lima faced it too. Her friends and family didn't understand her devotion to Christ. She wanted to enter a convent; her parents wanted her to get married. People admired her beauty; she feared that it endangered her relationship with Christ. Rose faced persecution in the way her family and friends rejected and ridiculed her piety—it interfered with what was expected of her. She was expected to use her beauty to find a wealthy husband and have a lot of kids.

I fear ridicule and rejection not just from people who do not believe but also from people who do believe, but believe differently. The former ridicule me for my belief; the latter reject the manner in which I believe as unorthodox at best, heretical at worst.

God is calling me, as God calls all of us, to be another Christ, and I will face opposition in following that call. Thus, the faith journey requires integrity—doing the right thing because it's the right thing to do. Unfortunately, integrity often invites rejection and ridicule.

But St. Rose reminds me not to fear rejection and ridicule because God's grace lives within me. I need to let that grace bloom into flowers of joy and delight, and freedom is the garden where those flowers grow.

Meditation: Rejected and Ridiculed

In this meditation, you will reflect on moments of rejection and receive Jesus' comfort. How do you comfort others when they feel rejected?

1. Ponder the following Scripture verse, allowing your mind to become calm and still and your breathing gentle and free:

   "Blessed are those who are persecuted for righteousness' sake, for theirs is the kingdom of heaven."

   —Matthew 5:10

2. Recall a time when you felt a particular grace. Think about the joys and delights it brought you. Give thanks to God for this grace. Keep this grace close to your heart.

3. Return to your day and walk through it hour by hour. Identify moments when you felt rejected or ridiculed.

What caused this persecution? Who were your persecutors? How did you respond to them?

4. Walk through your day again, this time identifying moments when you were the persecutor. When did you reject or ridicule others? What was the reason? How did you make others feel about themselves? How did you feel about yourself?

5. Reflect on the grace you identified above. Does it look or feel different in the face of ridicule or rejection?

6. Jesus knows a thing or two about being persecuted. Talk to him about your feelings. How does he comfort you? Ask for the grace to handle tomorrow's rejections with humility and grace, and ask for forgiveness for those times when you rejected others.

7. Close with this prayer or one of your own choosing: *St. Rose, pray for me that I may know the joys of God's grace. I ask this in Jesus' name. Amen.*

19

St. Philip Neri

1515–1595 • Feast Day: May 26

"Cheerfulness strengthens the heart and makes us persevere in a good life; wherefore the servant of God ought always to be in good spirits."
—St. Philip Neri

Some saints were really goofy.

Consider, for example, St. Philip Neri. He had been invited to a party with the most powerful people in the city of Rome. Philip was known as a living saint, and the host wanted to boast to Roman high society that he was friends with such a holy man. Knowing this, Philip decided to teach the host some humility. Philip showed up with his beard shaved off from one side of his face. The other guests must have thought him a fool; the host had impressed no one by inviting Philip.

Philip realized that a cheerful attitude makes space for us to play. But as I have gotten older, I have tended to restrict that space or eliminate it altogether. I might be too busy, or I have convinced myself that I need to put away such childish things. But when I stop playing, I push away the child in me.

Playfulness allows me to become a holy fool: I am free from being worried about what other people may think of me. I am free to let God's creative work be done through me. I am free to be a child at heart. That was the source of St. Philip Neri's cheerfulness.

St. Philip encourages me to be silly, to be a fool for God. After all, the word *silly* has the same root as the German word *selig,* meaning "blessed," which is the word Jesus used in the Beatitudes. Perhaps that is the greatest freedom of all: the freedom to be silly, to be children at heart.

Meditation: Playtime

In this meditation, you will remind yourself to be childlike by playing like a child.

1. Ponder the following Scripture verse, allowing your mind to become calm and still and your breathing gentle and free:

   "I thank you, Father, Lord of heaven and earth, because you have hidden these things from the wise and the intelligent and have revealed them to infants."

   —Matthew 11:25

2. Find something to play with, such as some modeling clay, a coloring book with crayons or colored pencils, a sticker book, or another toy. Spend some time playing with whatever it is. (If you don't have access to any toys, or if you feel silly doing so, imagine a time when you played as a child.)

3. After a few moments of playing, invite Jesus to play with you. How does he respond? Imagine playing with Jesus. What is playing with Jesus like? What do you learn about Jesus during this playtime? What do you learn about yourself?

4. How does it feel when playtime comes to a stop and Jesus has to leave? What does Jesus say to you? How do you respond to him?

5. Close with the following prayer or one of your own choosing: *St. Philip, pray for me that I always remain a child at heart. I ask this in Jesus' name. Amen.*

20

St. Josephine Bakhita

1868–1947 • Feast Day: February 8

*"The Lord has loved me so much: we must love everyone . . .
we must be compassionate!"*
—St. Josephine Bakhita

In the *Star Trek* franchise, there is a species of alien called the Borg. The Borg are cybernetic organisms that force other species to join their "hive mind" by assimilating them into their collective. They strip away everything that makes a person unique and individual. "Resistance is futile" was the last thing one heard when encountering the Borg.

St. Josephine would have disagreed: resistance is never futile. A native of Sudan, she was kidnapped at age seven, enslaved, abused, sold, and resold. She was finally bought by the Italian consul in Khartoum, Sudan, and taken to Italy, where she obtained her freedom. Despite all the indignities she suffered, Josephine's spirit was never broken. She always maintained her dignity as a child of God.

Our dignity comes from God: "So God created humankind in his image." (Genesis 1:27) Our value as human beings does not come from what we do or whom we associate with. Our dignity is not based on nationality, religion, or socioeconomic status. Our dignity comes from the simple fact that we are made in God's image. We are made out of love so that we may love.

And when we love someone, we respect their individuality and their dignity because they too are an image of God. To strip someone of their dignity—to deny them their human rights—is blasphemy.

As I reflect on the life of St. Josephine, I realize that protecting and advocating for human rights is a sacred act. Advocating for others' freedom is itself liberating—it frees me to love people less fortunate than myself. It is a solemn act of devotion.

Meditation: Loosen the Chains

In this meditation, you will reflect on human dignity and on how your dignity is linked to the dignity of others.

1. Ponder the following Scripture verse, allowing your mind to become calm and still and your breathing gentle and free:
   Submit yourselves therefore to God. Resist the devil, and he will flee from you.

   —James 4:7

2. We are made in the image of God—free to love and free to be loved. This freedom is the source of human dignity. Spend a moment giving thanks for those times when you

felt loved and those times when you showed love to others.

3. Spend a moment thinking about this question: *What does human dignity mean to me?*
   You do not have to come up with a formal definition; examples of dignity would suffice.

4. Review your day. When did you see such examples of human dignity? When was human dignity threatened?

5. Examine your role in these moments. Did you affirm another person's dignity or have your dignity affirmed? Were you the one who committed the abuse? Were you an enabler? Were you indifferent? How did the indignities affect you?

6. Talk to Jesus and tell him whatever is on your mind. What does he tell you about your dignity and the dignity of others?

7. Close with this prayer or one of your own choosing:
   St. Josephine, pray that I may always affirm my dignity and the dignity of others. I ask this in Jesus' name. Amen.

21

Mary, the Mother of God

First Century • Feast Day: January 1

"Here I am, the servant of the Lord; let it be with me
according to your word."
—Luke 1:38

My faith journey has been full of surprises. The surprise that has blessed me the most has been my devotion to the Blessed Virgin Mary.

She teaches me that God loves to surprise us. Imagine Mary's surprise when the archangel Gabriel greeted her. (Luke 1:26–28) Or how unexpected it was to hear Elizabeth welcoming her as the mother of the Lord. (Luke 1:43) She must have been amazed to meet the magi (Matthew 2:11–12) and shocked to hear Simeon's prophecy about her son (Luke 2:25–35). And she must have stood in awe when she found him in the Temple and Jesus told her that he was going about his Father's business. (Luke 2:49)

Unfortunately, I don't like to be surprised. I want to know what to expect so that I can prepare to respond the right way. I want to be in control of the situation. If I had met the archangel Gabriel, I would have wanted to know in advance how to respond. If I had known Elizabeth and Simeon were going to make such a fuss, I would have stayed under the radar. I would have wanted to know that the magi were coming so I could have moved to a more appropriate location for receiving guests. And if I had known all along that Jesus was in the Temple, I would have been too busy thinking of a punishment to inflict on him for disobeying me.

This is why freedom is so important: it allows us to let God be God; it allows us to let God surprise us.

And no one was more open to God's surprises than the Blessed Virgin Mary.

Meditation: Surprise!

In this meditation, you will reflect on how God has surprised you—and how you surprise God.

1. Ponder the following Scripture verse, allowing your mind to become calm and still and your breathing gentle and free:

   And my God will fully satisfy every need of yours according to his riches in glory in Christ Jesus.

   —Philippians 4:19

2. Imagine holding a gift-wrapped box in your lap. How big is it? What kind of paper is it wrapped in? Does it have a bow? A label on the box reads that it is for you, and it is from Jesus.

3. Pay attention to your feelings as you hold the box. How would you describe them? Are you anxious? Curious? Excited? Do you shake it to figure out what's inside?

4. You open the box. What's inside? Are you surprised? Disappointed? Share your responses with Jesus. How does he react to your response to his gift?

5. Now imagine that you are going to surprise Jesus with a gift of your own. What gift do you want to share with him?

6. You give your gift to Jesus. How does he respond to it? Is he surprised? Grateful? Annoyed? What does he tell you about this gift you have given him?

7. Close with the following prayer or one of your own choosing: *Holy Mary, Mother of God, pray to Jesus for me that I may always accept God's surprises with a grateful and open heart. Amen.*

Part Three
Pilgrimage

Our journey toward God is anything but a straight path. The journey has its ups and downs—there are times when we feel as if we are on fire with Christ's love; then there are times when God is noticeably absent. Sometimes we feel like the mythological figure Sisyphus, pushing a boulder up the side of the mountain, only to have it roll down once we get near the top. Other times our pilgrimage might feel like we're being spun around on a Tilt-A-Whirl.

The saints presented in this chapter will accompany you on your pilgrimage. Their lessons will help you express gratitude as you bask in the light of God's love and peace; they will help you remain hopeful during the dark nights of the soul.

The journey toward God also leads us toward our true self—the person God imagines you to be, a place that the Holy Spirit calls home.

22

St. Clare of Assisi

1194–1253 • Feast Day: August 11

"Draw me after you, / let us run in the fragrance of your perfumes, / O heavenly Spouse! / I will run and not tire, / until You bring me into the wine-cellar, / until Your left hand is under my head / and Your right hand will embrace me happily, / You will kiss me with the happiest kiss of Your mouth."

—St. Clare of Assisi, in the Fourth Letter to Agnes of Prague

We are all individuals, unique creations in the image of God. While we are all called to follow Christ, we do so in our own ways. Sometimes I want to sprint after him. Sometimes I want to hide from him. Sometimes I run after him, although it may seem to others as if I am standing still. And sometimes I get lost, discouraged, and tempted to give up.

St. Clare of Assisi knows what it's like to be on a long and winding pilgrimage toward God. Even though she joined Francis of Assisi to follow his life of gospel poverty—Francis called her his "Little Plant"—she wanted to do it in her own way. Clare had her own ideas about how she should follow Christ in his poverty. She wanted "to observe the Holy Gospel of our Lord Jesus Christ, by living in obedience, without anything of one's own, and in chastity." This was a radical departure from how women's religious communities were organized. Clare had to wait more than forty years and work with four different popes before the Church approved this way of living for her order, the Poor Clares.

She reminds me that my pilgrimage is not quick. It may be long and circuitous with many delays and detours. But when I reach my destination, I know I will be filled with joy.

Meditation: Draw Me a Map

In this meditation, you will reflect on how you approach Christ.

1. Ponder the following Scripture verse until your mind is calm and still and your breathing is gentle and free:
   Let your eyes look directly forwards,
   and your gaze be straight before you.
   Keep straight the path of your feet,
   and all your ways will be sure.

   —Proverbs 4:25–27

2. Imagine that you see Jesus in the distance. Even though you cannot make him out clearly, you know in your heart that it is him. How do you feel toward him? Rest for a moment with these feelings.

3. In your mind (or in your journal), draw a map toward Jesus. What routes are available? Which route is the most direct? Which route is the most dangerous, the one with the most obstacles?

4. Imagine journeying toward him along each of these routes. How do you feel when you reach him? Exhausted? Frustrated? Relieved? Excited?

5. Show Jesus your map. Ask him to point out which route he would have taken to reach you. Is it different from the one you took? Is it a route you didn't even consider?

6. Close with the following prayer or one of your own:
   St. Clare, help me find my way toward Christ. Amen.

St. Teresa Margaret Redi

1747–1770 • Feast Day: September 1

*"The merits of a good action can diminish when exposed to
the eyes of others who, by their praise or approval, give us
satisfaction or at least flatter our self-love and pride too much;
and that therefore it is necessary to be content to have
God alone."*

—St. Teresa Margaret Redi

St. Teresa Margaret Redi is overshadowed by other saints who
shared her Carmelite habit: Teresa of Ávila, John of the Cross,
and Thérèse of Lisieux. We could probably call her the "hidden saint." She entered a convent when she was seventeen and,
like her famous namesake, Teresa of Ávila, received visions
that drew her closer to God. Perhaps we would know more
about her had she lived longer—she died at the young age of
twenty-three.

I don't think she would have minded her obscurity. Teresa
wanted to keep much of her interior life hidden from others.
She did not want to attract attention to herself. Rather, she
wanted to imitate the Holy Family—humble, unassuming,
and just like everyone else. Despite having a rich and deep
prayer life, Teresa kept the gifts and graces she received from

God to herself, content to attend to sick people with love and compassion.

St. Teresa inspires me by challenging me. She challenges me to be quiet and unassuming; she challenges me to seek God's will by doing the will of others; she challenges me to "ask nothing, refuse nothing, but always be ready to do and to suffer anything that comes from His Providence." There is nothing special about my pilgrimage. Though our journeys may be distinct, we all journey from God toward God with God.

This helps me be a good traveling companion—I can be with another person on his or her journey. I don't need to tell them to take a different route than the one they are on.

Meditation: Just Like Me

This meditation will remind you that the graces you have received from God are not meant to make you feel good, special, or holy; these graces are to remind you that you are like Christ.

1. Ponder the following Scripture verse, allowing your mind to become calm and still and your breathing gentle and free:

    Do nothing from selfish ambition or conceit, but in humility regard others as better than yourselves.

    —Philippians 2:3

2. Spend a moment and think of a grace you have received. How does this grace make you feel about God? About

others? About yourself? Say a quiet prayer of gratitude for this grace.

3. Think of someone you love. What is a grace she or he has received? How does this grace appear in that person? How does that person use this grace? Slowly repeat the mantra "Just like me, she/he is blessed" several times as you imagine as many details as you can about that person.

4. Repeat this step, but think of someone you like, then someone you feel neutral toward, and finally someone you dislike. Repeat the mantra "Just like me, she/he is blessed" as you think about each person.

5. Imagine Jesus. How do these people appear to him? How does he model their graces? Repeat the mantra "We are like Christ" as you think of Jesus.

6. What arises in your heart as you meditate on these people? What feelings do you notice stirring within you? How would you describe them? Share your feelings with Jesus. How does he respond?

7. Close with the following prayer or one of your own choosing: *St. Teresa Margaret, pray that I seek not praise or flattery, but be content to have God alone. I ask this in Jesus' name. Amen.*

24

St. Anselm

1033–1109 • Feast Day: April 21

"The believer does not seek to understand, that he may believe, but he believes that he may understand: for unless he believed he would not understand."

—St. Anselm

On our pilgrimage toward God, it can be helpful to look at the starting point of our journey. We can ask, "Why do I believe what I believe?"

I remember asking myself the question, "Why should I believe in God?" when I was an undergraduate at Elmhurst College. I had to read about St. Anselm and his ontological proof for the existence of God in a theology course.

Anselm's argument went something like this: Let's define God as the greatest of all beings. Now, if God is something that we just made up, then God exists in our mind but not in reality. We should be able to imagine something greater than God. But we can't do that—remember, we defined God in such a way that there is no being greater than God. Therefore, if God exists in the mind, God exists in reality.

I think Anselm's argument contains a deeper truth about God: since God exists in my mind, the way I think about God changes the way I encounter God in the world. Similarly, the way I encounter God in the world changes the way I think about God.

Thus, my pilgrimage is a dance between my experience of God and my understanding of God. And like any good dancer, I'm less interested in being "correct" as I am in moving with harmony and grace.

Meditation: Time Lines

In this meditation, you will examine how your experience of God and your understanding of God have influenced each other.

1. Ponder the following Scripture verse, allowing your mind to become calm and still and your breathing gentle and free:

   When you search for me, you will find me; if you seek me with all your heart, I will let you find me, says the LORD, and I will restore your fortunes.

   —Jeremiah 29:13–14

2. Take a moment to think about some of the major points in your life. You might want to create a time line in your journal. Identify a beginning point (such as your earliest childhood memories) and an ending point (the present). Identify significant points in between, such as graduating from grade school, high school, or college, your first job, marriage, births, etc.

3. For each point in your time line, answer these questions:

   • How did your experience influence your understanding of God?

   • How did your understanding of God influence the way you experienced these moments?

   You might want to focus on a single point in your time line on each day of the week, so that you spend the week "walking" through your time line.

4. Imagine you are talking to Jesus. Share with him your thoughts and feelings about those moments in your life. How does he see them? What does he tell you about them? How did Jesus experience those moments with you?

5. Close with the following prayer or one of your own choosing: *St. Anselm, pray that I may always be mindful of God, think of God, and love God. I ask this in Jesus' name. Amen.*

25

St. Justin

c. A.D. 100–165 • Feast Day: June 1

*"But straightway a flame was kindled in my soul; and a love
of the prophets, and of those men who are friends of Christ,
possessed me; and whilst revolving his words in my mind, I
found this philosophy alone to be safe and profitable. Thus,
and for this reason, I am a philosopher."*
—St. Justin, *Dialogue with Trypho*

I once explained my faith journey to a friend of mine. While
I was baptized Presbyterian, I stopped practicing the faith by
the time I was in high school. While I believed in Truth, I
thought it more important to learn about this Truth than it
was to shackle it to some clever definition.

"I see," she said. "You were a seeker." I liked the sound
of that.

St. Justin was a seeker too. He studied the great philosophies
of his time—Stoicism, Pythagoreanism, and Platonism—to
understand what it meant to be happy. But it wasn't until he
learned about Christ that he found happiness.

Like Justin, I tried to find happiness by studying many different philosophies. But it wasn't until I met my wife and
witnessed how she celebrated her Catholic faith that I learned

the language necessary to describe what I had been searching for: faith, hope, and love.

My pilgrimage was similar to Justin's, and as I grow in my faith—that is, the more I let God be God—I am beginning to see it less as a journey from point A to point B.

Rather, I see my pilgrimage as a scavenger hunt where I discover God in all things.

Meditation: Seeking God

In this meditation, you will reflect on your images of God. How do you imagine God?

1. Ponder the following Scripture verse, allowing your mind to become calm and still and your breathing gentle and free:

   Now set your mind and heart to seek the LORD your God.
   —1 Chronicles 22:19

2. What is your current image of God? Spend a few moments creating this image of God in your mind. In what ways do you experience this image of God? For example, I may have an image of God as a forgiving father, and I experience this image of God in the sacrament of reconciliation.

3. Review your day and identify any moments of grace in which you felt God was present. What do these moments tell you about God? What image of God do they inspire?

How do these images compare and contrast with one another?

4. Share your images with Jesus. How would you describe God to him? How does he respond to your description? Does he correct you? Does he listen quietly? Does he ask questions to probe your understanding?

5. Close with the following prayer or one of your own choosing: *St. Justin, pray for me that I may devote my heart and soul to seeking God. I ask this in Jesus' name. Amen.*

26

St. Joseph the Worker

First Century • Feast Day: May 1

"It is certain that there was no worker's spirit so perfectly and deeply penetrated as the putative father of Jesus, who lived with him in the closest intimacy and community of family and work."

—Pope Pius XII, *Address to Italian Workers (May 1, 1955)*

"What do you do for a living?"

This question is usually the first thing someone asks me when we meet.

I like to answer, "I look for beauty in the world and affirm it." But then I'd be answering a different question: "What do I do *to live?*"

The difference between these questions is the difference between a career and a vocation. A career is how one makes a living—that is, how one provides for his or her needs and the needs of his or her family. A vocation, on the other hand, is the manner in which one loves God and loves others. St. Joseph had a career: he was a carpenter. But his vocation was to be the husband of Mary and the foster father of Jesus. He supported his family by working a trade; he loved God by loving, protecting, and serving his wife and foster son.

My vocation is the manner in which I travel as a pilgrim. When I know what that is, I don't really care what I do for a living, as long as it allows me to live my vocation.

And my vocation is to look for beauty in the world and affirm it.

Meditation: Career or Vocation?

In this meditation, you will reflect on the work that you do. Does it bring you closer to God?

1. Ponder the following Scripture verse until your mind becomes peaceful and your breathing is calm, gentle, and deep:

   Let the favor of the Lord our God be upon us,
   and prosper for us the work of our hands—
   O prosper the work of our hands!

   —Psalm 90:17

2. Recall one blessing from your workday—maybe a task that you accomplished, the companionship of a coworker or classmate, or the compliment of a boss or teacher—and give thanks to God.

3. Review your workday. What were the moments that made you feel more alive and connected to others and to God? What were moments when doubt and frustration left you feeling alone and disconnected? What patterns emerge? How is your work life-giving or life-draining?

4. Talk to Jesus about your work; Jesus understands the joys and frustrations of the worker. Imagine Jesus asking you, *"What do you do to live?"* How do you respond?

5. As you look forward to tomorrow, ask God for his blessing in the work you undertake to serve others and his kingdom.

6. Close with this prayer or one of your own choosing: *St. Joseph, pray for me that the Holy Spirit may guide me in discerning my true vocation. I ask this in Jesus' name. Amen.*

27

St. Bonaventure

1221–1274 • Feast Day: July 15

*"Concerning the mirror of things perceived through sensation,
we can see God not only through them as through his vestiges,
but also in them as he is in them by his essence, power,
and presence."*
—St. Bonaventure, *The Soul's Journey into God*

The world is immensely beautiful.

There is obvious beauty, such as the splendor of the rising sun or the delicate beauty of a rose. There is majestic, incomprehensible beauty, such as the Grand Canyon or the cosmic distance between our planet and the stars in the night sky.

And there is, of course, the beauty wrought by the imagination and genius of the human mind, whether it is oil on canvas, a sonnet that conveys the inexpressible meaning of love, or the elegant equation that can explain the mechanics of subatomic particles.

This beauty, according to Bonaventure, signifies "the invisible attributes of God." Just as we can learn a lot about an artist by studying his or her works, we can learn a lot about God by studying the things God created. And because God created them, they are good and beautiful. This lesson helps guard against fear and despair and keeps my mind open to find God in all things.

We can think of our pilgrimage as a tour through an art gallery, with Jesus as our guide. When we pay attention to the beauty that surrounds us all the time, we will find ourselves loving everything God created.

That is what the gospel is all about.

Meditation: Daily Beauty

This meditation will help you identify those moments of beauty in your day. How do these beautiful moments inspire hope?

1. Ponder the following Scripture verse until your mind becomes centered and your breathing becomes calm.
   God saw everything that he had made, and indeed, it was very good.

   —Genesis 1:31

2. Walk through your day, hour by hour. Look for those moments that you consider beautiful. Consider how each moment proclaims the goodness of God, the grandeur or splendor of God, and the reach of God. Give thanks to God for these moments.

3. Imagine that Jesus is standing next to you, looking at these moments of beauty as if the two of you were looking at a beautiful painting or another work of art at a museum or gallery. Do you stand with him in silence,

simply admiring the skill of the artist? Do you ask Jesus to explain the meaning of the work of art to you? Or does Jesus ask you to explain it to him?

4. As you look toward tomorrow, ask Jesus for the grace to see the beauty that exists in the world.

5. Close with this prayer or one of your own choosing:
St. Bonaventure, pray for me that I may always see what is good, what is true, and what is beautiful. I ask this in Jesus' name. Amen.

28

St. Frances Xavier Cabrini

1850–1917 • Feast Day: November 13

"We must not even desire that our pilgrimage on this earth be a short one because we do not yet know the infinite value of every minute employed for the glory of God."
—St. Frances Xavier Cabrini

When I was going through RCIA, I was working at an office a few blocks from Assumption Catholic Church in Chicago. During my formation, I made it a point to go to Mass at least once a week during my lunch hour.

One stained-glass window caught my attention: A woman dressed in black stands on a dock with a cross in her hand. Several immigrants gather around her. The Statue of Liberty is seen in the background, and Jesus Christ, pointing at his Sacred Heart, looks down from heaven.

Later I learned from one of the priests that the window depicts St. Frances Xavier Cabrini's arrival in the United States. Assumption Church has a close tie to her—she had worshiped at this parish, which was commissioned to minister to Italian immigrants.

Mother Cabrini served as a model for me as I was beginning my pilgrimage. She dreamed of traveling to the furthest reaches of the world. There was no place she didn't want to go; the world was too small for her. So she became a missionary—one of many "bearers of the love of Christ to the world"—and she immigrated to the United States, where she established schools, orphanages, and hospitals. Her love for God and her ability to surrender to that love made her pilgrimage a passionate one.

She reminds me that I need to have passion for my journey.

Meditation: A Passionate Journey

In this meditation, you will reflect on how passionate you feel about your spiritual journey.

1. Ponder the following Scripture verse, allowing your mind to become calm and still and your breathing gentle and free:

   I was glad when they said to me,
   "Let us go to the house of the LORD!"

   —Psalm 122:1

2. Recall a time when you went on a trip that you were really excited about. Where were you going? Who were you traveling with? How long were you going to be gone? What were you going to do there, and how did you prepare? Try to remember as many details as possible about this trip.

3. Imagine that you have the same sense of excitement and anticipation about your spiritual journey. Imagine going to church as if you were going to visit a close friend. Imagine prayer as the "suitcase" for your journey: What are the hopes, dreams, and questions you would pack in it? How would it affect your prayer life? How would it change the way you think about your faith? How would it affect the way you serve others? Do you see God differently? Yourself? Others?

4. Consider the obstacles that prevent you from approaching your spiritual journey with such enthusiasm. What are the obstacles to your prayer life? What are the obstacles that prevent you from being a person for others? What are the obstacles that prevent you from seeing yourself as God sees you?

5. Bring your concerns to Jesus. Imagine talking to him as you would a dear friend. What would you say to him? How does he respond to you? What graces do you need to follow him with enthusiasm and joy? Ask him for these graces, and, if you feel the need to ask him to forgive you, ask for his forgiveness.

6. Close with the following prayer or one of your own choosing: *St. Frances, pray that I may bear the love of Christ into the world. I ask this in Jesus' name. Amen.*

29

St. Catherine of Bologna

1413–1463 • Feast Day: May 9

*"But it is necessary that each who wishes to enter into this
battle never put down her arms, for her enemies never sleep."*
—St. Catherine of Bologna, *The Seven Spiritual Weapons*

"To win without fighting is best." So wrote Sun Tzu in the
ancient classic *The Art of War*.

St. Catherine of Bologna knew what fighting a spiritual
war—that is, our never-ending struggle against temptation—looked like. She fought against her own temptations—disbelief, sensual pleasures, feelings of despair and of
being forsaken by God. I, too, have a difficult spiritual struggle: I battle against apathy and despair; I fight against pride
and envy; I campaign against vanity and self-deception.

It seems that the enemy in this war is myself. How do I
fight such a war? If I'm constantly fighting against myself, I
will always be on the losing side.

Catherine explained that we can be victorious in this war if
we use seven spiritual weapons: 1) be diligent in doing good;
2) believe that we can never do anything truly good on our
own; 3) trust and have confidence in God; 4) meditate on the
events of Christ's life, especially his Passion and death; 5) be

mindful that we are mortal and are going to die; 6) be mindful of God's glory and the promises of heaven; 7) take to heart sacred Scripture.

We will face many battles on our pilgrimages. If we use the weapons described by Catherine, we will be victorious because we are not doing the fighting—we leave that to God.

Meditation: The Art of Spiritual Warfare

In this meditation, you will learn how to use some of the weapons described in The Seven Spiritual Weapons *by St. Catherine of Bologna.*

1. Begin by pondering the following Scripture verse until your mind becomes calm and still and your breathing gentle and free:
   Blessed be the Lord, my rock,
     who trains my hands for war,
     and my fingers for battle.

   —Psalm 144:1

2. What spiritual battle are you fighting today? Are you struggling with despair? Are you fighting against unbelief? Are you struggling with issues of trust in friends, family, institutions, or even the Church? We call these things temptations—things that lead us away from loving God, loving our neighbor, and loving ourself as God loves us.

3. Choose one or more of the following weapons:

   - diligence in doing good: do a good deed with intention and care;

   - belief that we can never do anything truly good on our own: each time you do a good deed, dedicate it to God;

   - trust and confidence in God: look at the graces God has blessed you with;

   - mindfulness of the events of Christ's life, especially his Passion and death: meditate on one of the mysteries of the Rosary;

   - mindfulness of our mortality: repeat the mantra, "I am dust, to dust I will return";

   - mindfulness of God's glory: meditate on what heaven might be like;

   - knowledge of sacred Scripture: read a verse from the Bible and ask yourself, "What difference does this make in my life?"

4. Use that weapon, and pay attention to the feelings that surround it. Does that weapon bring you consolation or desolation?

5. Spend some time talking to Jesus. What questions would you like to bring to him? Listen closely for his answers.

Jesus is teaching you how to use these spiritual weapons. Thank him for any insights he shares with you.

6. Close with this prayer or one of your own choosing: *St. Catherine, pray that I may know how to wield the weapons of love and peace. I ask this in Jesus' name. Amen.*

30

St. Juan Diego Cuauhtlatoatzin

1474–1548 • Feast Day: December 9

"Listen and understand, my humblest son. There is nothing to frighten and distress you. Do not let your heart be troubled, and let nothing upset you."

—Our Lady of Guadalupe, addressed to St. Juan Diego

To go on a pilgrimage, we must dare to surrender.

We have to surrender what we know for what we don't know. We have to surrender the comfort of safety and security for an unpredictable wilderness where we often feel helpless.

We would do well to imitate St. Juan Diego Cuauhtlatoatzin ("One Who Talks Like an Eagle").

Imagine his world for a moment. His people had just been defeated and humiliated by Spanish conquistadors. Missionaries came and said that the gods they worshiped—the gods that had helped the people understand the universe and their place in it—were false. Instead, they were presented with the God of love and mercy. Yet that message of love and mercy proclaimed by the missionaries was blatantly contradicted by the brutality of the conquistadors who worshiped the very same God.

In the face of this confusion, Juan Diego dared to accept something new—he accepted the message of Our Lady of

Guadalupe and did as she asked. He dared to begin a new journey, to begin a pilgrimage. He was willing to surrender the traditions of his people so he could begin walking toward the God of love.

The journey to God's kingdom will surely lead us out of our comfort zones, but we can take comfort in the example of Juan Diego.

Meditation: Discomfort

In this meditation, you will reflect on going beyond your comfort zone. What is God calling on you to leave behind?

1. Ponder the following Scripture verse, allowing your mind to become light and still and your breathing even and smooth:

   God chose what is low and despised in the world . . . so that no one might boast in the presence of God.

   —1 Corinthians 1:28,29

2. Review your day, looking for a moment when you had to go outside your comfort zone. What forced you out of your comfort zone? What did you have to let go of in order to start this journey? What feelings surrounded your departure—dread? resentment? eagerness? curiosity?

3. Where did this journey outside your comfort zone take you? How did you respond to the unknown? Did the journey expand your horizons by showing you new

perspectives, or did you long to retreat to the known and familiar?

4. Spend some time talking to Jesus about this journey. What does your journey look like from his perspective? Ask him to show you the graces that were present in it. Ask for the graces necessary to welcome such encounters as an opportunity to learn more about yourself, others, and the world.

5. Close with the following prayer or one of your own choosing: *St. Juan Diego, pray that I may always follow Jesus, even if it takes me outside my comfort zone. I ask this in Jesus' name. Amen.*

31

St. Thomas the Apostle

First Century • Feast Day: July 3

"Lord, we do not know where you are going. How can we know the way?"

—St. Thomas the Apostle, John 14:5

St. Thomas is my favorite apostle. He doubted as I doubted (and continue to doubt).

When I was growing up, I didn't understand people's belief in Jesus. I didn't *not* believe in Jesus—I accepted that there was a person named Jesus of Nazareth, a Jewish prophet who talked about the kingdom of God and inspired a religion. I just didn't necessarily share that devotion. My faith needed to be rooted in my experience—I wasn't going to accept the testimony of others. I wanted data.

Such cynicism, I realize, often makes me suspicious of other people's faith, especially those who are overly exuberant about it. In my doubt, I push them away.

When the other disciples told Thomas that they had seen Jesus risen from the dead, he basically said the same thing: "Show me the data." He needed to see for himself; he wasn't going to trust the testimony of others. Unlike me, however, Thomas didn't push the other disciples away. A week later, even though he had still not received the proof he had requested, Thomas was still with them. Only then did Jesus give Thomas the proof that he wanted. (John 20:20–27)

In my unbelief, the witness of others will provide me the data I need to put my doubts to rest. I shouldn't push them away; I need to travel with them.

Meditation: Doubts

In this meditation, you will wrestle with your doubts.

1. Ponder the following Scripture verse, allowing your mind to become calm and still and your breathing gentle and free:

   "I believe; help my unbelief!"

   —Mark 9:24

2. What are your doubts about your faith in God? When do you struggle with your belief in Jesus Christ? As you bring these doubts to mind, do not judge yourself; simply observe them.

3. What would ease your doubts? What grace do you think you need to help you believe?

4. Call to mind someone who does believe. Imagine spending time with this person. What do his or her actions tell you about God? What feelings arise in you as you imagine spending time with this person? What do you think these feelings are telling you?

5. Imagine Jesus appearing before you. How does he greet you? He offers you the grace that you requested. How do you respond to him?

6. Close with the following prayer or one of your own choosing: *St. Thomas, help me find Jesus even in my doubts. I ask this in Jesus' name. Amen.*

32

St. John of the Cross

1542–1591 • Feast Day: December 14

*"Oh, night that guided me, / Oh, night more lovely than
the dawn,
Oh, night that joined Beloved with lover, / Lover transformed
in the Beloved!"*
—St. John of the Cross, *The Dark Night of the Soul*

We will have to walk through some dark valleys on our journey toward God.

I remember going through one such valley. I was on my way to Mass, and I felt no desire to go. I was completely apathetic. That apathy continued throughout the liturgy: there was no Word of God, just words spoken poorly. There was no Eucharist, just stale wafers. There was no Body of Christ, just warm bodies.

God was totally absent. I was alone despite being surrounded by people who loved me.

St. John of the Cross calls such experiences of dryness when God is noticeably absent "the dark night of the soul." These experiences, he explains, are not meant to punish us. Rather, such dark nights are a grace—through them, we recognize our dependence on God, and, recognizing that dependence, we draw closer to God.

In other words, we have to go through the dark night of the soul to see the glory of God.

My feeling of dryness passed some time later when I received Holy Communion and I realized that I could never love God in the same way that God loves me. I wept for the first time in a long time—they were tears of love, joy, and gratitude.

That is the grace of the dark night of the soul.

Meditation: Night

In this meditation, you will imagine a dark night like that experienced by St. John of the Cross. This might be a very difficult meditation to do on your own. You may want to have a spiritual director lead you through it.

1. Ponder the following Scripture verse, allowing your mind to become calm and still and your breathing gentle and free:

   Even though I walk through the darkest valley,
      I fear no evil;
      for you are with me;
      your rod and your staff—
      they comfort me.

   —Psalm 23:4

2. Imagine that you are in a sunny valley, a place where you feel happy, free, and at peace. It is a place where you feel God's abundant grace all around you. Pay attention to your feelings in this place.

3. Imagine that a cell is built up around you. It is built from cold, hard stone; a thick door is locked from the outside; no light or sound can penetrate your cell. It is just you, the darkness, and the silence.

4. Try to stay in this darkness for as long as possible. You might want to stay there for only a minute or two at first, adding a minute on each subsequent meditation. If at any time you feel a sense of panic or anxiety, stop the meditation.

5. How do you feel in the darkness? How do you think God sees you?

6. The door unlocks. You see Jesus holding a small candle. The door closes behind him and locks. You and Jesus are sitting around the candle in the cold, dark cell. How do you react when you see him? How does he treat you? What do you say to him? What does he say to you? Imagine him leading you out of the cell. Where does he lead you?

7. Close with the following prayer or one of your own choosing: *St. John, pray for me as I walk through dark valleys, never forgetting that God is always with me. I ask this in Jesus' name. Amen.*

Part Four
Hospitality

Our pilgrimage leads us to God's dwelling place, which is in ourselves.

But what kind of home do we make for God? Do we make sure our home is clean? Do we make God feel welcome? Is God an unexpected guest, showing up when the house is a mess and we are embarrassed at the state of affairs?

The saints in this chapter will help us make space for the Holy Spirit. They offer us lessons on how to be welcoming and inviting—not only to God but also to our neighbors. Gracious hosts focus all their attention on their guests, attending to their every need. When we meditate on Christ, we attend to his only need: to be with us in love.

The temple of the Holy Spirit—which we are—is built not of the straw and twigs of intellect and reason but with the concrete and steel of love and kindness.

33

St. Benedict

c. 480–543 • Feast Day: July 11

---

*"In the reception of the poor and of pilgrims, the greatest care
and solicitude should be shown, because it is especially in
them that Christ is received."*
—St. Benedict, *The Rule of Benedict,* Chapter 53

I like to go backpacking. But after a few days of being exposed to the elements, sleeping on the hard ground in a tent, and eating trail mix, a hot meal, a long shower, and a dry bed can feel like heaven.

My spiritual journey is a lot like backpacking. There are times when I need to come out of the elements and find a safe, warm place to stay. I think St. Benedict understood this. Benedictine spirituality is known for its hospitality. "Let all guests who arrive," Benedict instructed his monks, "be received like Christ, for He is going to say, 'I came as a guest, and you received me.'" (Matthew 25:35)

I like to think I would receive everyone as Christ, but I know I don't. Sure, I may not object to being in the presence of someone I am not particularly fond of, just as long as they don't share their views on politics, religion, or sports. I will accept their presence but not their person.

That's not hospitality.

Hospitality means recognizing another person's dignity. It means listening to them, hearing their stories, and making them feel as if they are a welcome part of your life. Hospitality is an act of love. By welcoming another person into our lives with love and kindness, we are welcoming God into our hearts.

Meditation: Encounters

In this meditation, you will reflect on the degree to which you have welcomed other people, thoughts, and emotions with hospitality, kindness, and love.

1. Ponder the following Scripture verse until your mind becomes calm and still and your breathing becomes gentle and free:

   Lift up your heads, O gates!
   *   and be lifted up, O ancient doors!*
   *   that the King of glory may come in.*

   —Psalm 24:7

2. Take a moment and think of an encounter you had with something today that brought you joy. This could be a person, welcome news, or a pleasant thought or emotion. Thank God for this encounter.

3. Continue reviewing other encounters you had throughout the day—the pleasant ones and the unpleasant ones.

What about those encounters made them pleasant or unpleasant? Be objective; do not judge yourself—or them.

4. Pick one of these encounters and ask yourself: *Did I welcome it? Did I receive it with humility? Did I receive it with kindness and concern? Did I turn my back on it? Did I dismiss it with arrogance, disgust, or apathy?*

5. Imagine that you encounter Jesus. Does he come to you, or do you go to him? How do you welcome him? How does your reception of Jesus compare to the way you responded to the encounters you had throughout the day?

6. Imagine what your day would be like tomorrow if every encounter you had is like your encounter with Jesus. What graces would you need to realize that possibility?

7. Close with the following prayer or one of your own choosing: *St. Benedict, pray that I may receive everyone I meet as if they were Jesus Christ. I ask this in Jesus' name. Amen.*

34

St. Scholastica

c. 480–542 • Feast Day: February 10

*"See, I asked you, and you would not listen to me. So I asked
my Lord, and he has listened to me."*
—St. Scholastica, to her brother St. Benedict

Listening to another person might be the greatest act of compassion you can perform. It is the easiest way to welcome someone into your heart.

When I listen, I am accepting an invitation to become part of another person's story. I am saying, "Yes, your story is important and needs to be heard. I want to make your story part of my own."

But all too often, I find myself dismissive of other people. I might be too busy. I might not like what I hear; their story offends my sensibilities. When I dismiss another person's story, I am dismissing them. I rob people of their dignity by ignoring them.

Imagine how St. Scholastica must have felt. She had been enjoying her conversation with her brother Benedict—whom she only saw once a year—and she asked him to stay the night so they could continue their conversation. He refused, saying that his rule forbade it. Benedict ignored her story, which was really his own story, a story about how much he meant to her.

But God did not ignore her. A furious thunderstorm erupted that night that prevented Benedict from leaving.

God never ignores us. And since we are made in the image and likeness of God—if we are to imitate Christ—then we are called to listen to others.

Meditation: Do You Hear Me?

This meditation will help you develop a listening heart. If you don't listen well to others, you will struggle to listen to God.

1. Ponder the following Scripture verse, allowing your mind to become calm and still and your breathing gentle and free:

   You must understand this, my beloved: let everyone be quick to listen, slow to speak, slow to anger.

   —James 1:19

2. Review your day and identify the manner in which you listened to the people you encountered. Did you make yourself present to their stories? Did you find yourself ignoring them?

3. How did it feel to be invited into these stories? Did you recognize their joy or sorrow? Did you hear a plea of mercy? Did you share in their good news? Did you recognize your listening as an act of kindness or compassion?

Or did you only listen halfheartedly, out of a sense of obligation?

4. Did you ignore their stories? If so, why? Were you too busy? Did you think they did not merit your attention? How do you think they felt having been ignored? What graces may you have missed out on by not listening to them?

5. Invite Jesus into your story. Pay attention to how you imagine him listening to you. How might he be speaking to you through the stories you heard throughout the day?

6. Close with the following prayer or one of your own choosing: *St. Scholastica, pray that I may always listen with an open heart. I ask this in Jesus' name. Amen.*

35

St. Angela Merici

1470–1540 • Feast Day: January 27

"Remind them to behave well in homes (they go to), with good judgment, with prudence and modesty, and to be reserved and moderate in all things."
—St. Angela Merici, *Counsels Addressed to the Leaders*

Whenever we went to visit my grandma in Michigan, my sister, brother, and I were told clearly that we could not go to the nearby mill pond alone. I didn't understand why—the mill pond was a peaceful place for me to escape from my older siblings. Of course, now I understand why: my uncle had seen a friend drown there as a child. That rule was meant to keep me safe, and as a good guest, I followed that rule.

St. Angela Merici understood the importance of rules. She organized two dozen young women into a community dedicated to evangelizing through education. By the time of her death, Angela had established more than twenty communities. Today, there are communities all around the world. (We know them today as the Ursulines.)

Rules keep me safe, particularly from myself. And when I don't understand why I have to follow a particular rule, I would do well to heed Angela's counsel: "For it is better to follow what is certain, without danger, than what is uncertain, with danger."

Hospitality is not just something I offer to others; it is also something I receive. When I obey the rules, I am simply being a gracious and humble guest.

Meditation: Rules

In this meditation, you will reflect on the rules you are expected to follow. How do they help you accept the hospitality of others?

1. Ponder the following Scripture verse, allowing your mind to become calm and still and your breathing gentle and free:

   "Blessed are the meek,
   for they will inherit the earth."

   —Matthew 5:5

2. Think of welcoming a guest into your home. What rules do you make them follow? Why do you make them follow those rules? What purpose do those rules serve?

3. Imagine receiving two guests. One guest follows the rules, the other doesn't. How do these guests make you feel? How do you respond to the guest who doesn't follow your rules? Are you forgiving? Do you correct this guest?

4. Share your observations, thoughts, and feelings with Jesus. How would Jesus have behaved if he were one of the two guests? How would he have responded if he had

been the host? How does your behavior as the host compare to his?

5. Now recall a time when you were welcomed as a guest.
   What rules were you expected to follow? Which rules did
   you struggle to follow? How does your behavior as a guest
   compare to the behavior of the two imaginary
   guests above?

6. Share your observations, thoughts, and feelings with
   Jesus. How would he have responded if he were the guest?
   How does your behavior as a guest compare to his?
   Would your behavior have been different if Jesus were
   the host?

7. Spend some time talking to him about all this. Do any
   patterns of behavior emerge? If you feel the need to ask
   for forgiveness, ask for forgiveness. Ask Jesus for the grace
   to be a humble, gracious guest.

8. Close with the following prayer or one of your own
   choosing: *St. Angela, pray for me that I may always accept
   the hospitality of others with modesty and gratitude. I ask
   this in Jesus' name. Amen.*

36

St. Brigid of Ireland

c. 450–525 • Feast Day: February 1

"I should like a great lake of ale
for the King of Kings.
I should like the family of heaven
To be drinking it through time eternal."
—from a poem attributed to St. Brigid

Whenever people come to my house to visit, I like to offer them something to eat or drink. There is no better way to welcome them and make them feel at home.

I may not think much of this act; I can easily dismiss it as an expression of good manners and proper etiquette. But I see it as something much more profound: offering food and drink to visitors is an act of generosity, and if we are going to welcome God and others into our hearts, we need to be generous.

St. Brigid was known for her generosity. She gave away whatever she had—food, clothing, valuables—to anyone who asked. To practice generosity as St. Brigid did, I must surrender what I have to someone else. And in that act of surrender, I am free from the need to guard and protect what I have and can instead share what I have and who I am with the ones I love.

This is the lesson that St. Brigid teaches me: Offering someone something to eat or drink is not just a simple act of generosity; it is an act of great love.

Meditation: Refreshments

In this meditation, you will reflect on the importance of offering food and drink to people. How does Jesus feed and nourish you?

1. Ponder the following Scripture verse, allowing your mind to become calm and still and your breathing gentle and free:

   A generous person will be enriched,
   and one who gives water will get water.

   —Proverbs 11:25

2. Recall a time when someone offered you something to eat or drink. Who were you with? What was offered? Did you have to ask? Was it unexpected? Did you accept? As you think about this event, pay attention to the feelings that arise in you. Would you describe them as feelings of consolation or desolation?

3. Recall a time when you offered someone else something to eat or drink. Whom did you offer it to? What did you offer and why? Was it a sense of obligation? Was it done out of compassion? As you think about this event, pay attention to the feelings that arise in you. Would you describe them as feelings of consolation or desolation?

4. Imagine that Jesus comes to meet you. Where are you? What refreshments do you offer him? How does he respond? Imagine that you go to visit Jesus. Where is he? What refreshments does he offer you?

5. Finally, look forward to tomorrow. What "refreshments" will you offer to those who come your way? Will you offer kind, supportive words? Will you provide a listening ear? Remember that our daily bread nourishes our minds and our hearts, not just our bodies.

6. Close with the following prayer or one of your own choosing: *St. Brigid, may I always be generous in sharing what I have and who I am with others. I ask this in Jesus' name. Amen.*

37

St. Hildegard of Bingen

1098–1179 • Feast Day: September 17

"So all of creation is a song of praise to God."
—St. Hildegard of Bingen

St. Hildegard of Bingen was an abbess, a naturalist, a philosopher, and a mystic. She was also a composer—music formed the heart of her spirituality. Music, she taught, was a reminder of the beauty, joy, and harmony that existed before the Fall. Indeed, when I listened to her *Canticles of Ecstasy,* I could only imagine that this is what it must sound like to hear angels sing their unending hymns of praise to God.

The problem for me is that I prefer to listen to heavy metal. My playlist is filled with songs from bands like Metallica, Megadeth, Slayer, and Anthrax. No one can confuse their music with the songs of angels.

But if Hildegard is right, if "all of creation is a song of praise to God"—that is, if I can find God in all things—is it too much for me to think that I can find God's peace by listening to metal?

I don't think so. When I listen to heavy metal, my feelings—especially the darker ones, such as doubt, despair, sadness, and loneliness—find their voice. I can listen to them with compassion and share them with God, who then transforms them: my doubt is transformed into faith, my despair into hope, my sadness into joy, my loneliness into communion.

Welcoming the darkness that lurks in my heart is no easy task. I'd rather push that darkness aside and pretend it doesn't exist. But when I welcome that darkness, God's light will shine on it and transform it into something beautiful, something that praises God.

Meditation: Musical Interlude

This meditation will require music. Listen closely for God's love and compassion.

1. Ponder the following Scripture verse, allowing your mind to become calm and still and your breathing gentle and free:

   They sing a new song:
   "You are worthy to take the scroll
   and to open its seals,
   for you were slaughtered and by your blood you ransomed
   for God
   saints from every tribe and language and people and
   nation."

   —Revelation 5:9

2. Recall a time when you were troubled, a time when you were sad, lonely, afraid, angry, or despairing. What were the circumstances? Where are these emotions present in your body? Do you feel them in your hands? Are they present as a tightness in your shoulders or a lump in your throat? Attend to these emotions objectively, without judgment.

3. Play a song that comforts you, and listen to it attentively. What does the music say to you? How does it affect you? What changes do you notice?

4. When the song ends, talk to Jesus about what you're feeling and what the music said to you. How does he respond? What does he tell you?

5. Play the song again, and this time, ask Jesus to listen to it with you. How does he respond to it? How does the music move him? What insights does he share with you? Give thanks for spending time with him.

6. Close with the following prayer or one of your own choosing: *St. Hildegard, help me sing with creation in praise to God. I ask this in Jesus' name. Amen.*

38

St. Elizabeth of Portugal

1271–1336 • Feast Day: July 4

"God made me queen so that I may serve others."
—St. Elizabeth of Portugal

The phrase "peace through strength" always bothered me. "If I am strong," goes the thinking underlying this statement, "then nobody will dare mess with me, because whatever they do to me, I will do worse to them!"

But we can't ensure peace by threatening violence against others—it shows neither an understanding of peace nor an understanding of strength.

St. Elizabeth of Portugal teaches me that peace does not come through strength; peace comes through love. Her husband, King Denis of Portugal, had more children (seven) with other women than he had with her (two). Yet she remained a devoted wife, even educating the children her husband had with another woman. When her son, Alfonso, led a rebellion against the king, Elizabeth went to the front lines and convinced their armies to stand down.

Elizabeth worked so hard for peace because she saw God in each and every person. She could not help but love them and welcome them into her heart, no matter what indignities or abuse she might have suffered as a result.

Peace is not the absence of disputes or conflicts, nor is it simply the absence of violence. Peace is when love and kindness are in harmony. Therefore, if we are going to welcome the Holy Spirit into our hearts, we have to be people of peace.

Meditation: Peacemakers

In this meditation, you will reflect on how you bring peace into your daily life. Are you a peacemaker or do you sow the seeds of conflict?

1. Ponder the following Scripture verse, allowing your mind to become calm and still and your breathing gentle and free:

   "Blessed are the peacemakers,
   for they will be called children of God."

   —Matthew 5:9

2. Reflect on a fixed period of time, such as the previous day, week, or month. Review the events, moment by moment, as if you were watching a movie. Identify a single moment that you would label as a conflict, dispute, or fight. What was your role in it? Were you an instigator? Did you try to restore or preserve peace? Were you a bystander?

3. As you reflect on this conflict, what was required (or might have been required) for peace to be restored?

4. Talk to Jesus about this conflict. How does he see it? What do you think he would have done differently? What advice does he offer about how you should have handled the situation? If necessary, ask for forgiveness, or give thanks if that is appropriate.

5. Finally, ask Jesus for the grace to be a peacemaker. How can he help you bring peace to situations and the people who need it?

6. Close with the following prayer or one of your own choosing: *St. Elizabeth, may the peace of Christ flow through me and out into the world. I ask this in Jesus' name. Amen.*

39

St. Augustine of Hippo

354–430 • Feast Day: August 28

"Narrow is the mansion of my soul; enlarge Thou it, that Thou mayest enter in."
—St. Augustine, *Confessions*

Sometimes I think I would like to add a sunroom to our house. I could fill it with plants, and it would be large enough for me to practice tai chi and my wife to practice yoga. This room would be a sanctuary where I could sip tea and ponder Scripture or just be alone in the silence of God.

I suppose I ought to add a similar addition to my heart. I would like it to be more welcoming of people who cause me stress and anxiety, people who frustrate me, and people with whom I have serious disagreements. I want a warmer heart that is more forgiving and merciful.

St. Augustine enlarged his heart to welcome God. In his spiritual autobiography, *Confessions,* Augustine explained his conversion to Christianity. He resisted his conversion for years. Despite the constant petitions of his saintly mother, Monica, Augustine pursued his own desires, indulging in astrology, Manichaeism (a heretical sect that sought to separate matter from spirit), and sexual promiscuity. "Make me chaste, but not yet," he would pray.

Over time, Augustine learned how to examine his desires and evaluate whether they were from God and whether they led him to God. This is how he let God build an addition to his heart.

It's a good practice.

Meditation: Your Heart's Desires

In this meditation, you will examine your desires to see if they lead you to God. Consider celebrating the sacrament of penance and reconciliation after practicing this meditation.

1. Ponder the following Scripture verse, allowing your mind to become calm and still and your breathing deep and relaxed:

   But for me, it is good to be near God;
   I have made the LORD GOD my refuge.

   —Psalm 73:28

2. What do you desire? You may want to start with little desires—things you desired throughout the day, such as craving attention or praise from another person, an urge to respond to an insult or injury, or a taste for a good cup of coffee. These little desires may lead you to identify larger ones: a desire for fame, power, or comfort.

3. Pick one desire and attend to it. Imagine fulfilling that desire. Does it bring you feelings of consolation or desolation? Are those feelings long-lasting or are they fleeting?

4. Does this desire come from God? Does it lead you to God? Does it make you more faithful, hopeful, or loving? St. Augustine defined sins as those desires that do not come from or lead to God.

5. Tell Jesus about your desire. Listen to what he tells you. What would your faith be like if you desired Jesus with the same intensity? Ask for the grace to be free of those desires that do not come from or that lead you away from God. The sacrament of penance and reconciliation will reorient your desires toward God.

6. Close with the following prayer or one of your own choosing: *St. Augustine, pray that my heart finds its rest in God. I ask this in Jesus' name. Amen.*

40

St. Katharine Drexel

1858–1955 • Feast Day: March 3

"If we wish to serve God and love our neighbor well, we must manifest our joy in the service we render to Him and them. Let us open wide our hearts. It is joy which invites us. Press forward and fear nothing."
—St. Katharine Drexel

Sometimes when I celebrate Holy Communion, I think that we might be focused on the wrong miracle.

We are taught that during the consecration, the bread and wine are transformed into the body and blood of Jesus Christ. Truly, this is a miracle. But the bigger miracle is that when we partake in the body and blood of Christ during Holy Communion, *we* are transformed into the body and blood of Jesus Christ as well. Why do we always overlook that?

St. Katharine Drexel didn't. Her spirituality embraced the entirety of Christ's Body. She didn't limit the Eucharist to the celebration of the liturgy. She lived the Eucharist by being attentive to and responding to people's needs. To her, celebrating the Eucharist meant loving people as Christ loved them. This led Katharine to be a champion for racial justice, often facing racial prejudice (for example, she faced resistance to integrating parishes) and threats of physical violence (such as the time the KKK threatened to shut down the schools she founded to serve African Americans).

When we welcome people into our hearts with the same love and zeal with which we receive the Eucharist, we strive to make them feel at home with us and with Christ. After all, that is what the kingdom of heaven is: it is our common home where all are welcome.

Meditation: Give Us Our Daily Bread

In this meditation, you will reflect on how we are all Eucharist for one another. How do you give life to the world?

1. Ponder the following Scripture verse, allowing your mind to become centered and calm and your breathing gentle and free:

   "For the bread of God is that which comes down from heaven and gives life to the world."

   —John 6:33

2. Picture yourself looking in a mirror. How do you see yourself? What features stand out? Pray: "May I give life to the world. May God accomplish his work through me."

3. Bring to mind someone you love—a spouse, a child, a parent. Picture as many details about this person as you

can. Then pray, "May he/she give life to the world. May God accomplish his work through him/her."

4. Bring to mind someone you have no strong feelings for, either positive or negative. Create a clear mental image of this person and pray, "May he/she give life to the world. May God accomplish his work through him/her."

5. Bring to mind someone you strongly dislike, someone who brings you anxiety or distress. Create a clear mental image of this person and pray, "May he/she give life to the world. May God accomplish his work through him/her."

6. What feelings come up with each image and each prayer? Share these feelings with Jesus. What does he have to say about them? Give thanks for any insights you received, and ask for forgiveness if necessary.

7. Close with the following prayer or one of your own choosing: *St. Katharine, you loved all people as Christ loves us. May I do the same. I ask this in Jesus' name. Amen.*

41

St. Joseph Vaz

1651–1711 • Feast Day: January 16

"Hardly will one be able to do at the time of death what one has not done in life."

—St. Joseph Vaz

I like to sit at the back of the church during Mass. It's a physical reminder that I am on the outside edge of the inside.

One of the pillars of the Franciscan charism is the idea of minority—that is, going to the people who are on the margins of society. By expressing solidarity with the poor and powerless, we conform ourselves to Christ, who came into this world in poverty and humility.

This was a lesson that St. Joseph Vaz understood well. He welcomed the people who lived on the edges of society in Sri Lanka, and he made known the joy of the gospel to those who needed to hear it most: those whose human dignity was robbed by oppression, fear, hunger, and poverty.

By going to the periphery of society, Joseph Vaz ignored the racial, ethnic, and religious boundaries that divided the people of Sri Lanka. By ignoring those boundaries, he upset the social order that was responsible for putting people on the margins. And it resulted in him suffering the persecution that naturally follows when one ignores established boundaries for the sake of love.

Sitting in the back of the church reminds me that I am to make a home for people who are not welcome—in society, in the Church, or in my heart.

Meditation: The Margins

This meditation will take you to the periphery of your life. Where do you see Christ in the people who live on the margins?

1. Ponder the following Scripture verse, allowing your mind to become calm and still and your breathing gentle and free:

   [He] emptied himself,
   taking the form of a slave,
   being born in human likeness;
   And being found in human form.

   —Philippians 2:7

2. Review your day, searching for those people who were on the periphery, those people you ignored. Maybe it was a person begging for change at the street corner. Maybe it was a coworker who was not important enough to have his or her opinions or ideas count for anything. Or maybe it was a person who has the "wrong" ideas.

3. Bring one of these people to the forefront of your imagination. Try to recall every detail about them. What were

they wearing? What expression was on their face? What were they doing when you encountered them? Imagine what this person's desires might be. How are they similar to what you want?

4. Reflect on how you treated this person. Is this how you would like to have been treated if you were in his or her shoes? What can you do to be aware of people who are on the margins? What can you do to be with them there? How can you give them a voice?

5. Imagine if this person were Jesus. Would you have treated him or her differently? What does Jesus have to say about being treated in this way? If necessary, ask for forgiveness, and ask for the grace necessary to be present to people on the margins.

6. Close with this prayer or one of your own choosing:
St. Joseph, help me love people who are ignored and marginalized. I ask this in Jesus' name. Amen.

42

St. Teresa of Ávila

1515–1582 • Feast Day: October 15

"I believe we shall never learn to know ourselves except by
endeavouring to know God."
—St. Teresa of Ávila, *The Interior Castle*

I first learned about the practice of contemplation when I read a biography of Teresa of Ávila. She reminds me that, as a Secular Franciscan, prayer and contemplation are the source of all I am and all that I do. But she also cautions me that prayer cannot come at the expense of charity. Prayer and contemplation, if not directed toward love of neighbor, can easily become narcissistic.

In her book *The Interior Castle,* Teresa describes the soul as if it were "resembling a castle, formed of a single diamond." This castle is made up of seven rooms, or "mansions." The first three rooms form the outer courtyard. In these rooms, we struggle with worldly concerns and temptations as we try to discern God's will and perform acts of charity. As one moves into the three rooms of the inner courtyard, worldly concerns fade away as we experience the consolation of drawing closer to Christ, until we enter the inner sanctum of the seventh room: the bridal chamber where one experiences union with Christ.

I love the imagery of *The Interior Castle*. First, it reminds me that my soul is a place of great beauty and dignity. Second, *The Interior Castle* invites me to roam its many rooms, to see what treasures lie within its walls.

This is, after all, the place the Holy Spirit calls home. (1 Corinthians 6:19)

Meditation: A Walk through Your Castle

In this meditation, you will find where God dwells in you.

1. Ponder the following Scripture verse, allowing your mind to become calm and still and your breathing gentle and free:

   Do you not know that your body is a temple of the holy Spirit within you, which you have from God, and that you are not your own?

   —1 Corinthians 6:19

2. Each day of the week, spend time in one of the rooms of your interior castle. As you go through each room below, imagine what it "looks" like. How is it decorated? Does it have windows? Is it cluttered and dusty or clean and well-kept? Pay attention to the details.

- **The First Room:** When did you find yourself consumed by worldly concerns or anxieties? These are the times when God seemed far from your thoughts.

- **The Second Room:** When did you see or hear God's word? It may have been a Scripture reading, but it may also have been an unspoken word of kindness, generosity, or love that you witnessed. This is the room where we begin to discern God's will.

- **The Third Room:** When did you perform an act of mercy or charity for yourself or others? This is the room of penance—that is, the room where we perform concrete actions that draw us closer to God.

- **The Fourth Room:** At what times did you feel consolation—that is, when did you feel joy and grace well up from within you? Note that this consolation is not the kind that would result from a good act on your part (such feelings dwell in the third room). Rather, this feeling of consolation is spontaneous, unexpected, and effortless.

- **The Fifth Room:** In which moments did you notice a surrender to God's will? This surrender might be marked by feelings of wholeheartedness, detachment, and quiet contentment, even in the face of difficulties.

- **The Sixth Room:** When were you conscious of God's glory? This is a subtle, indescribable awareness that Christ is near you. It may also be accompanied by a feeling of desolation, a feeling that everything is worthless when compared to this glory.

- **The Seventh Room:** When did you have an epiphany—some great insight into the nature of your relationship with the Holy Trinity? This is a moment of rapture, a moment when you have been struck blind and dumb with the love of God.

3. Spend some time talking to Jesus. How do you describe that room to Jesus? How does he describe that room to you?

4. Close with the following prayer or one of your own: *St. Teresa, pray for me that I may always see myself as precious in God's eyes. I ask this in Jesus' name. Amen.*

Part Five

Loving Knowledge

St. Paul writes that "Love is patient; love is kind; love is not envious or boastful or arrogant or rude. It does not insist on its own way; it is not irritable or resentful; it does not rejoice in wrongdoing, but rejoices in the truth. It bears all things, believes all things, hopes all things, endures all things." (1 Corinthians 13:4–7)

This is a high standard to live up to, but the lessons I learned from the saints in this chapter show us that not only can we find this kind of love, but we can learn how to live it as well. Love, as St. Paul describes, is a new way of living that allows us to find God in all things.

When we rest in the loving knowledge of God—that is, when we rest in the knowledge gleaned from the experience of loving God—we will see that the kingdom of heaven is at hand.

That is the good news we need to share.

43

St. Teresa of Calcutta

1910–1997 • Feast Day: September 4

*"Let us conquer the world with our love. Let us interweave
our lives with bonds of sacrifice and love, and it will be
possible for us to conquer the world."*
—St. Teresa of Calcutta, *No Greater Love*

I remember when we had to put down our beloved dog. She
was a fourteen-year-old Siberian Husky named Shakira. Our
house seemed so empty afterward. So did our hearts. Our pack
was incomplete. And so, a few months later, we adopted two
huskies, Allison and Happy, from a local rescue organization.
A few weeks after adopting them, I said to my wife, "I am so
glad that we adopted them. They have brought so much love
back into our house."

They brought love back into our house not because they
loved us but because they gave us something to love.

St. Teresa of Calcutta taught me that love has to have an
object. Love is not some abstract feeling or emotion—it is a
concrete act of kindness and generosity that brings joy and
beauty into the moment. Such love comes from within—it
comes from our participation in the life of the Trinity.

"Loving," St. Teresa wrote, "must be as normal to us as living and breathing."

St. Teresa's life was a lesson in love—love for God and love of neighbor. We do not need to do spectacular deeds; all we need to do is show compassion to those who suffer, and Jesus will do the rest.

Meditation: Love Them Anyway

This meditation will help you show love to people you might consider unlovable. No matter what people may do to you—for good or ill—love them anyway.

1. Ponder the following Scripture verse, allowing your mind to become calm and still and your breathing gentle and free:
   For God so loved the world that he gave his only Son.
   —John 3:16

2. Think of someone you know whom you think of as unreasonable or irrational. Imagine yourself talking to Jesus about this person. What does he tell you? What would you like to ask him? How might you forgive this person?

3. Think of a time when you were honest and sincerity made you vulnerable. What was the situation? What emotions arise in you when you recall your vulnerability?

Imagine yourself talking to Jesus about your vulnerability. What does he tell you? What would you like to ask him?

4. Think of a good deed that you did that was unrecognized and forgotten. What emotions arise in you as you think of this deed? Do they encourage or discourage you from doing good in the future? Imagine yourself talking to Jesus about this. What does he tell you? What would you like to ask him? What good deeds might you do tomorrow?

5. Think of a time when you experienced failure in spite of your best efforts. What emotions arise in you as you recall this failure? Imagine talking to Jesus about this failure. What does he tell you? What would you like to ask him? Where will you find the strength to continue giving your best effort to the things you do?

6. Close with the following prayer or one of your own choosing: *St. Teresa, pray that I may be free to love all those I meet. I ask this in Jesus' name. Amen.*

44

St. Catherine of Siena

1347–1380 • Feast Day: April 29

*"GOD: By the effect of this virtue, the soul draws to herself all
the other virtues, which, as has been said, are all bound
together in the affection of love."*
—St. Catherine of Siena, *Dialogue of Divine Providence*

I went to a retreat in which we had to develop our own personal rules for living. My personal rule was to affirm the beauty in the world, nurture a sense of wonder in the little things, know true and perfect joy, and live each moment in gratitude.

This rule is short on specifics, I know, but upon reflection, I noticed a particular virtue that God had hidden in it: playfulness. But how do I use this virtue in a way that leads me to be more like Christ? The *Dialogue of Divine Providence,* a record of a conversation St. Catherine of Siena had with God the Father, offers me some helpful advice.

God the Father explained to Catherine that the virtues "are brought forth in the love of neighbor." These virtues are given to us for the sole purpose of loving one another: "love of Me and of her neighbor are one and the same thing, and, so far as the soul loves Me, she loves her neighbor, because love towards him issues from Me." My playfulness becomes a virtue when it helps me love others and let myself be loved by others, for it is through love that the soul is united with God.

Meditation: Virtues

In this meditation, you will reflect on how virtues help you love and be loved.

1. Ponder the following Scripture verse, allowing your mind to become calm and still and your breathing gentle and free:

   They go from strength to strength;
   the God of gods will be seen in Zion.

   —Psalm 84:7

2. Think of a virtue you have been blessed with. A virtue is a habit or disposition to do good. Virtues allow us to give the best of ourselves in any situation. You can also think of a virtue as a mental state that leads you toward a feeling of consolation.

3. How do you use this virtue to show love, kindness, and compassion to yourself, someone in your family, a close friend, someone you don't know, and someone who makes you frustrated, afraid, or angry?

4. If you discover that this virtue does not help you show love, compassion, and kindness toward all these people,

then it is not a virtue. Ask the Holy Spirit to help you discover what your virtue might be:

- Recall a time that you distinctly remember feeling consolation.

- What were you doing at the time? What was your mental state like?

- Review other times you felt this way and shared a similar state of mind. Do any patterns emerge? Do you notice any habits?

- Repeat step three with this newly discovered virtue.

5. How do you use this virtue to show Jesus your love for him? How does Jesus use this virtue himself? Spend a few moments talking to Jesus about this. Share with him any obstacles that prevent you from using this virtue. Ask him for the grace to be virtuous.

6. Close with the following prayer or one of your own choosing: *St. Catherine, pray that I may follow the footprints of Christ and walk from virtue to virtue. I ask this in Jesus' name. Amen.*

45

Blessed Miguel Augustin Pro

1891–1927 • Feast Day: November 23

"If I meet any long-face saints [in heaven], I will cheer them up with a Mexican hat dance!"
—Blessed Miguel Augustin Pro

I am a cheerful guy. "Bring joy and laughter to every situation" is my personal credo.

Blessed Miguel Augustin Pro might have shared a similar credo—he had a great sense of humor. But he is not remembered for that. Miguel Pro is most often remembered for his martyrdom. He is remembered for celebrating the sacraments in secret because the Mexican revolution outlawed public worship. He is remembered for being falsely accused of attempting to assassinate the president of Mexico. And he is mostly remembered for his famous last words as he faced a firing squad: "¡Viva Cristo Rey!" or "Long live Christ the King!"

Miguel is not as well-known for the jokes he played on his friends. Not many people know that he liked to draw cartoons—one is of a mischievous cat that had put a muzzle on a puppy; another is of a man who fell off a horse because the horse he was riding tripped while jumping over a fence.

Miguel Pro understood the importance of humor: Life is hard, and humor is a great way to help relieve people of their suffering. I can think of no better way to show love and kindness to someone than by making them laugh.

Meditation: Solace

In this meditation, you will reflect on cheerfulness and humor. How does God cheer you up?

1. Ponder the following Scripture verse, allowing your mind to become calm and still and your breathing gentle and free:

   A glad heart makes a cheerful countenance,
   *   but by sorrow of heart the spirit is broken.*

   —Proverbs 15:13

2. Recall a time that was challenging or difficult for you. Imagine as many details as possible. Who was involved? What were the circumstances? What feelings do you associate with that time?

3. As you reflect on that time, ask yourself one (or both) of the following questions: 1) What was something that made you laugh during that time? 2) What cheers you up now when you think about that difficult time? As you consider one of these questions, do you notice any changes in your emotions?

4. Share your difficult time with Jesus. What does he do or say that cheers you up? Ask him how you might bring gladness and cheerfulness to people who are struggling. Thank him for this grace.

5. Close with the following prayer or one of your own choosing: *Blessed Miguel, pray for me that I may always have a glad and cheerful heart. I ask this in Jesus' name. Amen.*

46

St. Boniface

c. 680–754 • Feast Day: June 5

"Do you then, beloved, rejoicing in the hope of a heavenly fatherland, hold the shield of faith and patience against all adversity of mind or body."

—St. Boniface, in a letter to his friend Bugga, an abbess

I like to think that, someday, I will be remembered for great deeds.

Consider the example of St. Boniface. We remember the "apostle to the Germans" because of his great deeds: he organized the Church in Germany, revitalized it in France, founded monasteries, and brought the gospel to the Germanic tribes.

As great as those deeds are, they are not what stand out to me. Rather, it was a simple letter of encouragement Boniface wrote to an old friend, Bugga. She had resigned as the abbess of a monastery and was suffering from, as Boniface described it, "weighty troubles." He goes on to offer her support, comfort, and consolation.

In the middle of his great and important work in Germany, Boniface took time to write a letter filled with love, kindness, and compassion to a beloved friend. He didn't rely on prayer alone.

Whenever I see someone who is hurting or suffering, I am often content to say, "I'll pray for you." St. Boniface reminds me that I ought to do more: when I see someone who is suffering, I need to stop what I'm doing and offer my support and loving presence.

That is the kind of great deed I want to be remembered for.

Meditation: Sympathy

In this meditation, you will offer love and kindness to those who are suffering.

1. Ponder the following Scripture verse, allowing your mind to become calm and still and your breathing gentle and free:

   Suffering produces endurance, and endurance produces character, and character produces hope, and hope does not disappoint us.

   —Romans 5:3–5

2. Reflect on your day. Where have you faced challenges, troubles, or adversity? What has caused you pain? What feelings come up as you recall these afflictions? Locate those feelings somewhere in your body.

3. Imagine receiving a letter from Jesus. What words of encouragement, support, and consolation does he share

with you? Imagine writing a letter back to him. What would you write?

4. Reflect on your day again. This time, identify someone who might have been suffering from some sort of affliction. What kindness, support, or consolation could you show that person?

5. Close with the following prayer or one of your own choosing: *St. Boniface, may I never consider myself too busy or too important to offer love and kindness to those who suffer. I ask this in Jesus' name. Amen.*

47

St. Peter Faber

1506–1546 • Feast Day: August 2

*"Therefore seek the right devotion to God and to his saints
and you will easily find the right relation to your neighbors,
toward friend and foe!"*
—St. Peter Faber, *Memoriale No. 143*

If you are familiar with the cartoon *Family Guy,* you might recall a character named Buzz Killington. He was a stodgy old British gent with a dry sense of humor. In one episode, he ended a raucous frat party by asking, "Now who here likes a good story about a bridge?" The life was sucked out of the party and it ended abruptly. The show's main character, Peter Griffin—who was partying the hardest—sighed with painful disappointment.

I, on the other hand, love good stories about bridges, particularly stories about the people who build them. Bridge builders make good peacemakers.

St. Peter Faber was one such bridge builder. One of the original Jesuits (Peter attended the University of Paris with Ignatius of Loyola and tutored him in Latin grammar), Peter worked to revive the Catholic faith that was being challenged by Martin Luther and other leaders of the Protestant Reformation.

However, Peter refused to see them as enemies. He saw them as wounded individuals who needed comfort. He saw himself as the Good Samaritan—given the choice between being an agent of God's wrath or God's mercy, he always chose to be an agent of mercy.

If I want to be a bridge builder like St. Peter Faber, I need to remember that all of us are good. Despite our failings and all the bad that we do, there is always good in each of us. Knowing that, I can reach out to others and make peace with love and kindness.

Meditation: Conversation

In this meditation, you will use your imagination to show love and compassion to your so-called enemies.

1. Ponder the following Scripture verse, allowing your mind to become calm and still and your breathing gentle and free:

   "And you, child, will be called the prophet of the Most High; for you will go before the Lord to prepare his ways, to give light to those who sit in darkness and in the shadow of death, to guide our feet into the way of peace."

   —Luke 1:76, 79

2. Imagine someone you would consider an "enemy." This might be someone you've disagreed with; it could be someone who consistently antagonizes you; it might be someone you perceive as a threat. Bring to mind as many details about this person as possible, and pay close attention to your feelings as you do so.

3. Enter into a conversation with this person. As you talk, listen patiently. Try to understand where this person feels pain, sorrow, and loss. As you listen, pay attention to your feelings toward this person. Do you notice a shift in them?

4. How do you reach out to this person to show comfort? Do you share soothing words of healing? Do you desire to embrace this person with love and compassion? How has your image of this person changed? How do you end your conversation with him or her?

5. Imagine now that you are talking to Jesus. What would you tell Jesus about this person's suffering? How would you want Jesus to view this person? What does Jesus tell you to do for him or her?

6. Close with the following prayer or one of your own choosing: *St. Peter, pray that I may always seek to change hearts, not minds. I ask this in Jesus' name. Amen.*

48

St. Maria Goretti

1890–1902 • Feast Day: July 6

"I invoke her for you, dear young people, so that she may help
you to choose good always, even when it is to your cost."
—Pope Emeritus Benedict XVI, General Audience 7 July 2010

St. Maria Goretti is most often remembered for the virtue of chastity: when a boy named Alessandro raped her, she resisted and he stabbed her fourteen times. "With splendid courage," Pope Pius XII said about her, "she surrendered herself to God and his grace and so gave her life to protect her virginity. . . . Parents can learn from her story about how to raise their God-given children in virtue."

But we are missing the more important parts of the story, such as when she forgave Alessandro on her deathbed. Or when she visited Alessandro in a dream and handed him a bouquet of flowers. Or when Alessandro, upon his release from prison, sought forgiveness from Maria's mother, Assunta. Or when Alessandro, who had become a Franciscan friar, attended the canonization Mass of the girl he had murdered and cried tears of joy.

St. Maria's great virtue was not chastity. It was charity. This charity comforted her sorrowful mother and moved her murderer to seek forgiveness.

When we live in charity—when we are loving and kind—nothing is more important than to forgive others so they might know peace. That is the lesson I learn from St. Maria Goretti.

Meditation: Forgiveness

In this meditation, you will practice forgiveness and reconciliation.

1. Ponder the following Scripture verse, allowing your mind to become calm and still and your breathing gentle and free:

   "Father, forgive them; for they do not know what they are doing."

   —Luke 23:34

2. Think of a person you need to forgive. Why does this person need forgiveness? As you think about him or her, what feelings do you notice? Fear? Anger? Hatred? Sorrow? Compassion?

3. Imagine this person in a prison cell. Imagine him or her suffering from anger, regret, and bitterness. If you could give this person a gift that would provide him or her some level of comfort, what would you give?

4. Imagine yourself bestowing this gift to this person with the words, "I forgive you." Do you give generously? Do you give hesitantly? Are you guarded? Do you refuse to give anything at all?

5. Have a conversation with Jesus. Share with him your experience in forgiving this person. What does he tell you about your resistance, if any? What graces do you need to be able to overcome any resistance to forgiving those who hurt you? Ask Jesus for these graces.

6. If you notice an obstacle to forgiveness, consider offering up this obstacle to God during the sacrament of penance and reconciliation.

7. Close with the following prayer or one of your own choosing: *St. Maria, pray that I may always choose to forgive others, no matter how hard it may be. I ask this in Jesus' name. Amen.*

49

St. Maximilian Mary Kolbe

1894–1941 • Feast Day: August 14

"A single act of love makes the soul return to life."
—St. Maximilian Mary Kolbe

St. Maximilian Mary Kolbe taught me an important lesson about love: the sacrifices we make for others show us how much we love them.

While he was a prisoner in the Auschwitz death camp, a man named Franciszek Gajowniczek was going to be executed. Franciszek began to cry for his wife and children—he would never see them again. Maximilian offered his life to the commandant in exchange for Franciszek's. The exchange was made, and Maximilian was executed. I'm sure he would have approved of the exchange: Franciszek survived and lived to be ninety-three years old.

When I think about some of the nasty, extended arguments I've had with my brother and sister over the years—some of which resulted in our not speaking with one another for years—I realize that I wasn't willing to make a very important sacrifice: I was unwilling to give up the idea that I had to be right and imagine the possibility that they were right.

Maximilian sacrificed his life for a man he barely knew in a Nazi death camp. And I struggle to sacrifice my vanity for my own siblings by giving them the benefit of the doubt.

I should follow St. Maximilian's example and learn how to be willing to make sacrifices for others. I can start small—no one is asking me to give up my life. Even small sacrifices, if done out of love, can give life.

Meditation: Self-Sacrifice

In this meditation, you will identify moments when you sacrificed yourself for others.

1. Ponder the following Scripture verse, allowing your mind to become calm and still and your breathing gentle and free:

   No one has greater love than this, to lay down one's life for one's friends.

   —John 15:13

2. Take a look at your day and identify individual acts of sacrifice. When did you give up something of yourself so that someone else could benefit? It doesn't matter how small your sacrifice may seem to you; you never know how much your sacrifice may have benefited that person.

3. What compelled you to make this sacrifice? Was it an act of love and compassion? Did you do it without thinking?

4. Imagine what your sacrifice looked like from the point of view of the person who benefited from it. How do you appear from this perspective? Do you see yourself any differently?

5. Take a moment and imagine that you are at the foot of Jesus' cross. How might you imitate the love with which he sacrificed all of himself for you?

6. Close with the following prayer or one of your own:
St. Maximilian, pray that I may offer my love and kindness to those who suffer, no matter the cost. I ask this in Jesus' name. Amen.

50

St. Francis de Sales

1567–1622 • Feast Day: January 24

"If love is the milk of life, devotion is the cream thereof; if it is a fruitful plant, devotion is the blossom; if it is a precious stone, devotion is its brightness; if it is a precious balm, devotion is its perfume, even that sweet odour which delights men and causes the angels to rejoice."

—St. Francis de Sales, *Introduction to the Devout Life*

I was at dinner with some friends when the topic of religion came up, and someone asked if I was a devout Catholic.

"No, not really," I said.

Another friend called me out. She reminded me that I am a Secular Franciscan, work for a Catholic publishing company, pray the Rosary every day, and am a catechist at my church. She also pointed out that I had just come from daily Mass.

"Yeah, you're not devout," she said. "You're Super Catholic!"

After reading *Introduction to the Devout Life* by St. Francis de Sales, I realize that none of those things are good measures of my devotion. Devotion, Francis explained, "is neither more nor less than a very real love of God." Francis used the metaphor of fire and flame to describe this relationship: "love being a spiritual fire which becomes devotion when it is fanned into a flame." Out of love, we obey God's commandments; we fulfill them out of devotion.

There is a gift greater than God's love, however: it is the gift of devotion. If I want to live a devout life, I need to let my love for God grow without restraint, for love begets love.

Meditation: Devotion

In this meditation, you will practice devotion.

1. Ponder the following Scripture verse, allowing your mind to become calm and still and your breathing gentle and free:

   Those who eat of me will hunger for more,
   And those who drink of me will thirst for more.

   —Ben Sira 24:21

2. Think of a time when you experienced God's goodness. What did it feel like to experience God's love? Where were you? Who was present? What was the time of day? As you bring this event to mind, pay close attention to your feelings. How would you describe them?

3. Recall a good deed that you did. Imagine if you had done this deed while experiencing these feelings. What effect does this have on how you remember this deed?

4. Recall a time of suffering, a time when you might have been sorrowful, angry, fearful, or anxious. Imagine

experiencing this suffering while accompanied by these feelings of God's love. What effect does this have on how you remember this time?

5. Looking back on these memories together, ask yourself, "What difference does love make?" Talk to Jesus about this. What does he tell you? What would tomorrow look like if you loved with the same kind of devotion you held throughout this meditation? Ask Jesus for whatever you need to do this.

6. Close with the following prayer or one of your own choosing: *St. Francis, pray that through the gift of devotion, I may know the Lord's peace and love. I ask this in Jesus' name. Amen.*

51

St. Faustina Kowalska

1905–1938 • Feast Day: October 5

"O Jesus, make my heart sensitive to all the sufferings of my neighbor, whether of body or of soul."
—St. Faustina Kowalska, *Diary, 692*

"Be merciful," Jesus tells us, "just as [also] your Father is merciful." (Luke 6:36) This makes me wonder, though: what is mercy and how can I be merciful?

To help me answer this question, I turn to St. Faustina Kowalska. Jesus entrusted her to carry his message of mercy and forgiveness. She recorded Jesus' message of divine mercy in her diary, which has been translated into more than twenty languages.

So what do I learn from this apostle of Divine Mercy?

First, to be merciful, Faustina teaches, I need to trust in God. Faustina realized that the basis of mercy is trust. "The soul desirous of more of God's mercy should approach God with greater trust; and if the trust in God is unlimited, then the mercy of God toward it will be likewise limitless." (*Diary,* 1489)

Second, to be merciful, I need to take on the sufferings of others. Faustina prayed to take on the temptations others were suffering so that they would know peace: "I desire to struggle, toil, and empty myself for our work of saving immortal souls." (*Diary*, 194)

Finally, to be merciful, I need to be joyful. Faustina recognized that God delighted in her: "You are My joy," Jesus told her in her mystical visions. (*Diary*, 27) Knowing that God delighted in her, despite her many failings, she was able to delight in others.

When I trust in God, when I am compassionate, and when I am full of joy, I will know mercy, because it is in those moments that I have encountered God.

What, then, is mercy? Mercy is wherever God meets me.

Meditation: Mercy

In this meditation, you will reflect on mercy.

1. Ponder the following Scripture verse, allowing your mind to become calm and still and your breathing gentle and free:

   Bless the LORD, O my soul,
   and do not forget all his benefits—
   who forgives all your iniquity,
   who crowns you with steadfast love and mercy.

   —Psalm 103:2,4

2. Think of someone who is suffering. It may be someone close to you; it may be an acquaintance, or it may be

someone you've never met. You may also want to think of a group of people who are suffering. Try to imagine as many details about this person (or group) as possible.

3. Turn your attention to your breathing. As you inhale, imagine that you are breathing in all of this person's (or group's) suffering. Hold your breath for a second, and let that suffering dissipate through your body. As you exhale, breathe out love, compassion, and mercy. Repeat this cycle. If your mind is distracted by wandering thoughts, gently return your attention to the person or group and continue to breathe in their suffering and exhale compassion.

4. Gently shift your attention to Jesus. Imagine that he is standing in front of you. Two rays come forth from his heart: one ray is red, representing his blood; the other ray is white, which represents water. Imagine these rays pouring over you and the people you were praying for.

5. Listen to Jesus as he says, "Happy are you who dwell in the shelter of my mercy." What feelings come over you as you hear his words? What do you think God is trying to tell you?

6. Close with the following prayer or one of your own choosing: *St. Faustina, pray that I may be merciful as my heavenly Father is merciful. Jesus, I trust in you. Amen.*

52

St. Thérèse of Lisieux

1873–1897 • Feast Day: October 1

"Jesus does not expect great actions from us but simply surrender and gratitude."
—St. Thérèse of Lisieux

I consider St. Thérèse of Lisieux to be my first spiritual teacher. My wife had received a statue of St. Thérèse as a gift for her bridal shower. Not being Catholic at the time, I read that Thérèse was known as "The Little Flower."

So I placed some flowers next to her.

But many years later, I began to understand the brilliance of her "little way"—the way of doing ordinary things with extraordinary love. Her "little way" reminds me to pay attention to what I am doing in the moment and attend to that moment with great love. When I focus on doing little things—walking the dog, drinking a cup of coffee, or washing the dishes—with great love, I can be indifferent to my goals, expectations, and accomplishments, which are invariably self-centered. Instead, I am free to live life without an agenda other than to love.

"My vocation is love!" she declared. I realize now that placing flowers next to her was an act of love. It wasn't a great act—I didn't become a Carmelite; I didn't rush off to become

Catholic; I didn't even finish the biography that came with the statue—but it was a simple act of love.

After all, the simple act of giving flowers is a great way to say "I love you."

Meditation: The Little Meditation

In this meditation, you will reflect on how the things you do bring you closer to God.

1. Ponder the following Scripture verse, allowing your mind to become centered and still and your breathing gentle and free:

   "Be still, and know that I am God!
   I am exalted among the nations,
   I am exalted in the earth."

   —Psalm 46:10

2. This meditation focuses on the *now* by paying attention to moments as you experience them, whether that moment is an action, a thought, or an encounter. Every now and then throughout your day, stop and pay attention to what you are doing.

3. Ask yourself if this particular moment is bringing you consolation—does this moment make you feel whole or complete? Does it bring out the best in you? Or does this particular moment bring you desolation—do you feel

isolated, alone, and incomplete? Is the moment bringing out things that you would rather keep hidden?

4. What would it look like or feel like to love whatever it is you are doing in that moment?

5. Imagine Jesus is with you in this moment, helping you do whatever it is you might be doing. What would you like to share with him? What does he have to say?

6. Close with the following prayer or one of your own choosing: *St. Thérèse, pray that I always remember that the greatness of my deeds is measured only by the love with which I do them. I ask this in Jesus' name. Amen.*

Epilogue

In reading about the saints in this book, I learned a few facts about them. I learned a little bit about their lives and their times. I learned a little bit about their charisms—the particular gift God had given them to be like Christ—and their spirituality.

But most importantly, I learned about myself. I learned that what motivates me is love. I learned that love makes its home in my heart, and it propels my journey toward God. I learned that love gives me the freedom to surrender myself to love.

And I hope these little lessons from the saints help you see yourself, others, and the entire world through the eyes of love.

When we make love the center of our being, we can hold the tension in the world—we can hold the good with the bad. The saints show us how to reorient our lives so that we can be patient, kind, joyful, hopeful, and compassionate. They show us how to be saints ourselves.

This is how we can affect change in the world and play a part in building God's kingdom in heaven here on earth.

Saints Among Us

"Here are my mother and my brothers! Whoever does the will of God is my brother and sister and mother."

—Mark 3:34–35

I chat online with one of my best friends almost every day.

"Tell me a story about a saint," she asked one day. She knew I had been writing this book and was of great help with my drafts. (Like me, she is also an editor.)

I was writing the meditation on St. Peter Faber at the time. I copied the few paragraphs I had written and shared them with her.

"Seriously?" she asked. "You made him a saint for that? No offense, but that's nothing. That's just being a kind and understanding person."

She had a point. The saints are not special. They are not superheroes with magic powers. They are not idealized versions of what people should be. They were real people who chose to take the gospel seriously. The saints remind us that it is possible to live the gospel: It is possible to be poor in spirit and turn the other cheek. It is possible to love those who hate you. It is possible to forgive. The saints show us the many different ways to listen to Jesus and follow Mary's admonition to "do whatever he tells you." (John 2:5)

Any time I show love and compassion, I am a saint. Whenever I am kind and gentle, I am a saint. Whenever I show patience and understanding, I am a saint. Whenever I am meek and humble, I am a saint.

My goal is not to be canonized someday—my goal is to live the gospel today. If I do that, I can look in the mirror and see a saint every day!

Meditation

In this meditation, you will seek the saints who continue to walk among us and reflect on what they teach us about Christ.

1. Ponder the following Scripture verse, allowing your mind to become calm and still and your breathing soft and free: *Be imitators of me, as I am of Christ.*

    —1 Corinthians 11:1

2. Of the people you know, choose one whom you consider to be saintly. How is this person generous, joyful, gentle, peaceful, faithful, modest, kind, good, and disciplined? Call to mind as many details about him or her as possible. Pay attention to your feelings. Does thinking about this person bring forth feelings of consolation or desolation?

3. What does this person teach you about what it means to follow Christ? How is this person an example of living the gospel? How might you apply these lessons to your own circumstances?

4. Enter into a conversation with Jesus. What does he tell you about this person? What questions do you have for Jesus? What answers does he give you? What does he tell you about the feelings you have toward this person? If there is anything you would like to ask Jesus, now is the time to ask.

5. Close with the following prayer or one of your own choosing: *Lord Jesus, may I look to others to inspire me to follow you, and may I inspire others to follow you. Amen.*

A Lesson from Your Favorite Saint

"The feasts and memorials of the Mother of God and the saints call us to praise God for what he has accomplished in them and to imitate their virtues."

—United States Catholic Catechism for Adults

A friend of mine complained that I didn't include St. Paul in this book.

"You *have* to include St. Paul!" he protested one day as we ate lunch. "How could you not include him?"

"He just didn't speak to me like the others," I explained.

I'm sure there are many other saints who speak to you but don't speak to me. But, even though they chose to remain quiet here, you can still meditate on their virtues daily. You don't need to become an expert on your favorite saint—I am certainly no expert on any of the saints in this book. You just need to learn a little bit about them before you can begin to imitate their virtues.

The template below will guide you on how to listen to what your favorite saint has to say so that you can do what he or she did, in your own unique way.

Meditation

In this meditation, you will listen to your favorite saint.

1. Spend a few moments centering your mind until it is calm and still and your breathing is gentle and free. You may wish to focus on a particular Scripture verse or pray the Lord's Prayer slowly.

2. Bring to mind your saint. You might want to read about him or her from one of the following resources:

   - Alban Butler, *Lives of the Saints* (TAN Books, 1995)
   - Bert Ghezzi, *Voices of the Saints* (Loyola Press, 2000)
   - James Martin, *My Life with the Saints* (Loyola Press, 2007)

- Miguel Arias and Arturo Pérez-Rodríguez, *Saints of the Americas* (Loyola Press, 2007)
- Sarah Gallick, *The Big Book of Women Saints* (Harper-Collins, 2007)

3. What lesson does this saint teach you about following Christ? How did you apply that lesson today? How will you apply that lesson tomorrow? Examine your feelings as you reflect on this saint's lesson. Do these feelings draw you closer to God?

4. Enter into a conversation with Jesus, or if you prefer, enter into a conversation with your patron saint. What questions do you have? What do you learn about God, others, or yourself?

5. Close with the following prayer or one of your own choosing: *Lord Jesus, may the saints always lead me to you. Amen.*

Prayer Notes and Thoughts

_____

_____

_____

_____

_____

_____

_____

_____

_____

_____

_____

_____

_____

_____

_____

_____

_____

_____

_____

_____

_____

_____

Acknowledgments

St. Ignatius said that ingratitude is the greatest of sins. Without gratitude, we easily forget that life and everything in it is a gift.

So first and foremost, I would like to thank my beautiful and inspiring wife: None of this would have been possible without you. Cathy, thank you for believing in me.

I am also grateful to Loyola Press for giving me this opportunity: Thank you for allowing me to chase this dream of mine. In particular, I want to thank Joe Durepos and Denise Gorss. This book was their idea. I hope I did not disappoint them. I need to thank Joe Paprocki, Tom McGrath, Vinita Wright, Rosemary Lane, and Beth Renaldi. They have been so helpful to me in finding my voice, not only for this book, but in my spiritual life as well.

I would also like to thank Sr. Diane Przyborowski, OSF. She taught me how to be present to God and always reminds me that meditation is not magic but very hard work. And I would like to thank my two very close friends, Kris Fankhouser and Kathy Osmus. Kris read many of my early drafts over Frappuccinos at Starbucks; his observations inspired me to unpack my thoughts and distill their meaning. Kathy asked me daily to tell her a story about a saint. She kept me honest and diligent. I would also like to thank my sister, Kathleen March; she listened to me as I struggled to bring everything together.

Finally, I would like to thank the good people at Resurrection Catholic Church in Wayne, Illinois. They brought me into the Catholic Church and continue to walk with me. The youth of Resurrection deserve extra thanks—they always remind me to stay a kid at heart.

About the Author

Bob Burnham is a Secular Franciscan and a spiritual director. He works as a freelance editor and writes about the spirituality of commuting on his blog, www.mtransit.org. He lives with his wife Cathy in Bartlett, Illinois.

Continue the Conversation

If you enjoyed this book, then connect with Loyola Press to continue the conversation, engage with other readers, and find out about new and upcoming books from your favorite spiritual writers.

 Visit us at **www.loyolapress.com** to create an account and register for our newsletters. Or scan the code to the left with your smartphone.

Connect with us through:

 Facebook
facebook.com
/loyolapress

 Twitter
twitter.com
/loyolapress

 YouTube
youtube.com
/loyolapress

Also Available

An Ignatian Book of Days
$12.95 | 4145-1 | PB

A Simple, Life-Changing Prayer
$9.95 | 3535-1 | PB

God Finds Us
$9.95 | 3827-7 | PB

Reimagining the Ignatian Examen
$9.95 | 4244-1 | PB

Ignatian Spirituality Online
www.ignatianspirituality.com

Visit us online to

- Join our *E-Magis* newsletter

- Pray the Daily Examen

- Make an online retreat with the *Ignatian Prayer Adventure*

- Participate in the conversation with the dotMagis blog and at **facebook.com/ignatianspirituality**

3-Minute Retreat

3 minutes a day can give you 24 hours of peace.

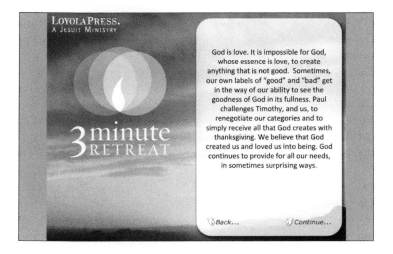

The *3-Minute Retreat* invites you to take a short prayer break at your computer. Spend some quiet time reflecting on a Scripture passage and preparing your heart and mind for the day ahead.

Sign up to receive a daily invitation to reflect, delivered to your inbox every morning.

**Join the conversation at
facebook.com/3MinuteRetreat**